Protest, Culture and Society

Kathrin Fahlenbrach, Department of Communication and Media Studies, University of Halle Wittenberg, Germany.

Martin Klimke, German Historical Institute, Washington, DC / Heidelberg Center for American Studies (HCA), University of Heidelberg, Germany.

Joachim Scharloth, Department of German, University of Zurich, Switzerland.

Protest movements have been recognized as significant contributors to processes of political participation and transformations of culture and value systems, as well as to the development of both a national and transnational civil society.

This series brings together the various innovative approaches to phenomena of social change, protest and dissent which have emerged in recent years from an interdisciplinary perspective. It contextualizes social protest and cultures of dissent in larger political processes and socio-cultural transformations by examining the influence of historical trajectories and the response of various segments of society, political and legal institutions on a national and international level. In doing so, the series offers a more comprehensive and multi-dimensional view of historical and cultural change in the twentieth and twenty-first century.

Voices of the Valley, Voices of the Straits

How Protest Creates Communities

Donatella della Porta and Gianni Piazza

Berghahn Books
New York • Oxford

First published in 2008 by
Berghahn Books
www.berghahnbooks.com

Library of Congress Cataloging-in-Publication Data

Della Porta, Donatella, 1956-
  Voices of the valley, voices of the straits : how protest creates
communities / Donatella della Porta and Gianni Piazza.
      p. cm. -- (Protest, culture and society ; v. 1)
  Includes bibliographical references and index.
  ISBN 978-1-84545-515-6
1. Protest movements--Italy. 2. Communities--Italy. 3. Environmentalism-
-Italy. 4. High speed trains--Environmental aspects--Italy--Susa Valley.
5. Bridges--Environmental aspects--Italy--Messina, Strait of. I. Piazza,
Gianni, 1963- II. Title.

  HN475.5.D457 2008
  307.1'40945--dc22

                                                    2008026633

British Library Cataloguing in Publication Data
A catalogue record for this book is available from the British Library
Printed in the United States on acid-free paper

ISBN 978-1-84545-515-6 hardback

Contents

Acknowledgments

Many people helped us to write this book. First of all, we are grateful to the activists on the No Tav and No Ponte protest campaigns, who trusted us with their memories of highly intense experiences and their reasons for acting. We hope this book can help them, among others, make their voices heard.

We are also grateful to those who helped us with the research on which this volume is based. In particular, Massimiliano Andretta and Eugenio Pizzimenti who carried out the interviews and collected documents on the protests in Val di Susa.

Different versions of chapters of this book have been presented at conferences at the European University Institute in Fiesole, the Universitat Autònoma de Barcelona, the ECPR joint sessions in Nicosia, and the annual conference of the Società Italiana di Scienza Politica in Bologna. We learned from comments and criticism made by colleagues on all these occasions.

We are finally grateful to our respective partners, Herbert and Egle, who supported and tolerated us with love and patience during this long and hard work.

The geographical distance notwithstanding, the two authors cooperated intensively during the research in the field, the analysis of the results, and the writing of this book. Each chapter is in fact a comparative analysis of the two cases, built upon Donatella della Porta's knowledge of the Val di Susa campaign and Gianni Piazza's expertise on the No Ponte protest. Although sharing responsibility for the complete book, the final drafting of the manuscript has been divided as follows: Donatella della Porta has written chapter 1.1., chapter 3 and chapter 4 (excluding 4.6 to 4.8); Gianni Piazza chapter 1.2., chapter 2, chapter 4.6 to 4.8, and chapter 5.

Florence – Catania, November 2007

D. d. P. – G. P.

to Federica, Marcella, Stefano, Raffaele, Lorenzo and Till,
to their future

to Maria and Vincenzo,
in memoriam

Chapter 1

Local Conflict between Interest and Identity: an Introduction

For a twinning of No Tav–No Bridge

For the sovereignty of inhabitants from north to south there emerges a single struggle: a moratorium on large-scale public works, cancellation of the Objective law, and participatory planning for infrastructural transport projects. We have affirmed and repeated that the pacific revolt of the inhabitants and mayors of the Val Susa concerns all those who love their territory and in particular those who in recent years have opposed the realisation of damaging and useless large-scale public works, from the Tav to the Mose to the Bridge on the Messina Straits … the peaceful revolt of the inhabitants and mayors of Val di Susa has placed the issues of democracy and justice at the centre of the political debate in our country. What has been defined as a particularist interest, whether of the community of Val di Susa or that of the Straits, is instead the expression of sovereignty of the people that inhabit the territory, reclaiming their legitimacy to decide their own future and that of their children … the struggle in Val di Susa is the same as the struggle against the Messina Bridge, against the incinerators, against nuclear generators; it is the same commitment as those that want to slow down, who have begun to notice the signals of crisis in the planet, who propose a sober future, who consider the limited resources of the planet and think that all mankind has the right to benefit from what the earth offers. (DME 17)

The flyer that promotes this alliance between the far north and far south of Italy is signed by the Rete No Ponte ("No Bridge Network") and the Rete Meridionale del Nuovo Municipio ("Southern Network for a New Municipalism"). While the former unites various committees and associations from the area of the Messina Straits opposed to the construction of a bridge between Calabria and Sicily, the latter seeks to involve both local politicians and citizens in the practices of participatory democracy. The twinning is proposed with the No Tav committees and Mayors of Val di Susa (on the border with France), who oppose the construction of a 57 km tunnel as part of a new high-speed rail line. This twinning pact is signed on 17 January 2006 at Condove in Val di Susa, while on the following day in both Reggio Calabria and Messina (the cities in Calabria and Sicily on opposite sides of the Straits) a national protest is announced for 22 of January, which will take place in Messina and mobilise 20,000 people, including a solid delegation from the Val di Susa.

In this monograph we shall analyse these two protest campaigns, which social sciences would generally classify as being related to locally unwanted land use (LULU), considering them in light of the principal hypotheses in the sociological literature on local conflict, as well as locating them within the literature on global movements.

1. Nimbyism or Social Movements?
How to Explain Protest Campaigns

Protest campaigns against large-scale public works usually take place within a local context. If the aggregation of needs and interests in a given territory is certainly not a new phenomenon, in the 1990s we *see* growing analytical focus on new forms of protest, which have been portrayed as limited and localised. It has been observed that those seeking to defend the quality of life in a limited territory tend to oppose public works that are seen as either compromising ecological equilibrium (e.g. refuse incinerators) or compromising public security (e.g. insertion of unwanted social groups in their territory). The presence of localised conflicts has met with great concern, given the multiplication in both these types of LULU protests in recent years (della Porta 2004a).

1.1. The Local Dimension

Local conflicts are usually seen in the sociological literature (and more generally) as being motivated by a "not in my backyard" (Nimby) syndrome, associated with a conservative behaviour and egotistical resistance to social change. In public policy analysis local opposition is often associated with dangerous "free-riderism": the refusal to pay the necessary costs to attain public goods. The committees of citizens mobilised against large-scale public works have been defined as a "specific organisational form that accompanies the Nimby syndrome" (Bobbio 1999: 196), characterised by the "limited nature of their demands ... as they do not fight for 'great causes' but simply to defend a specific and defined material interest" (Buso 1996: 197). Given the concentration of the real or perceived threat in a given territory, these protests often succeed in mobilising residents by appealing to a strong sense of injustice as well as to fears of material threat. Above all, these protests are capable of obtaining the support of local politicians, who (fearing the loss of electoral support) pledge "to move away the public bad, opening in another territory the difficult question of allocation" (della Porta

2004a: 11). On the basis of these observations, research on local opposition to large-scale public works has proposed changes in decision-making procedures, through the involvement of citizens in the implementation of "high-impact" projects in their territory. The objective is to overcome the "why here?" syndrome (Bobbio and Zeppetella 1999) not only by improving transparency in public decision-making, but also by elaborating criteria to attribute LULU projects, legitimising the process through consensual procedures, if not necessarily a consensual outcome.[1]

In the course of our research the term Nimby frequently appears, above all as an accusation directed towards those who protest against either High-Speed Trains (Tav) or the Bridge on the Messina Straits. If the citizens committees and activists proudly proclaim their belonging to a territory, those who promote large-scale public works stigmatise their local egotism, claiming to represent progress for the many rather than the few. A proponent of this argumentation is the centre-left President of the Piedmont regional government, Mercedes Bresso, who maintains that "it is important that we overcome the 'not in my back yard' syndrome, it brings us nowhere" (R 20/11/05), as well as the former centre-right Minister for the Environment, Altero Matteoli, who stigmatises the "egotism of an instrumentalised protest" (R 4/11/05). More recently the Secretary of the Democrats of the Left (Piero Fassino) has declared that in Val di Susa:

> We must face a problem posed not only in Italy but in any country every time a large-scale public work is proposed, whether it is a power station or an incinerator or a high-speed railway. Diffidence and rejection have become increasingly common reactions: build it anywhere but not in my backyard. Faced with this behaviour we must avoid two mistaken reactions, that is, either becoming paralysed by the fear and risks involved in a project (even before verifying if there are any risks), or reacting as if these fears and concerns are not worthy of being addressed. We must not react to these situations in an ideological fashion ... the Tav is not the ultimate symbol of an Imperialistic State of Multinationals as some believe. It is a project that is necessary for the economic and social development of our country and Europe. (R 14/2/06)

As in this case, the accusations of Nimbyism often merge individual egotism and ideological reactions, extreme rationality and obscure fears. This interpretation of the Nimby syndrome has been contested both by activists and by the social science community, the latter observing that "Nimbyist discourses tend to place residents in an illegitimate position" (Jobert 1998: 73). In fact empirical research on local oppositions has indicated a complex reality, with citizens' committees characterised by a diverse capacity or will to present their particular claims within a more comprehensive framework (della Porta 2004a: 19). As research on several Italian cities has suggested, these claims tend to become intertwined with the themes of defending quality of life, the artistic or natural heritage, health or social integration (Sebastiani 2001; Andretta 2004). Of the eighty-nine citizens' committees recorded in a study of six Italian cities, only around a quarter (26.2 per cent) mobilised using a Nimby discourse (i.e. single issues in a restricted territory), while the others tended to amplify the territorial and thematic range of their claims (della Porta 2004a: 22).

1.2. Social Movements and Environmentalism

In contrast to a Nimby reading of the situation, sociological research has often interpreted local conflict as an expression of different types of social movements (della Porta 2003b). In the discourse of those who protest, the defence of the local fauna is accompanied by a more general defence of natural resources. From this point of view, local conflicts can be interpreted as an evolution in the ecologist movement, characterised by a growth (in numbers, resources and legitimacy) of environmental organisations, with the diffusion of an environmental awareness in public opinion (although concentrated on specific themes), as well as an extension of activities beyond traditional organisational networks or environmental discourses (della Porta and Diani 2004). Although Italian environmental organisations are weak in economic resources and political influence (when compared with those of other European countries), even these have increased in number and support from public opinion. In the process of becoming more institutionalised, they have engaged less in dramatic forms of protest, dedicating themselves more to informational and educational activities among the population, as well as the provision of different types of services. While environmentalism has become a value, environmental actions have become more conventional and hence less visible in the public sphere.

In contrast to the 1970s and 1980s, a main role in the mobilisation of the protest is now played by citizens' committees, that is, organised but weakly structured groups of citizens that unite on a territorial basis and use forms of protest to oppose interventions that they claim to be damaging for the quality of life in their territory and which they want improved (della Porta 2004a: 7). Local protests are changing the image of environmentalism: from the "post-materialist" issues shared by a "new bourgeoisie" with high levels of education, to the claims of underprivileged groups, above all in degraded areas, where implants of high environmental impact (e.g. incinerators) are often built. In these conflicts environmental associations are usually present, although they often have difficult relations with other organisations based in the territory (della Porta and Rucht 2002). During the course of protests against the construction of new airports (Rucht 1984; Griggs and Howarth 2002) or military installations (Touraine et al. 1981, 1983) these diverse actors have interacted and reciprocally influenced each other.

The protests in Val di Susa and the Messina Straits have a strong environmental dimension. In both cases there is opposition to public works that are seen as damaging to the ecological equilibrium of a particularly delicate territory, whether mountainous valleys or coastal strips. In our two conflicts we find the definition of the problem (Tav or bridge) in terms of a threat to the environment, and we note the participation of the largest environmental associations (from the World Wide Fund for Nature, WWF, to Legambiente), as well as the formation of citizens' committees that are active in communes or neighbourhoods where the works are planned. Although frequently adopting different strategies and despite some tensions, environmental associations and citizens' committees have collaborated in both these protest campaigns. Despite the emphasis on defence of the environment and the health of inhabitants, the protests in the Val di Susa and the Straits cannot be defined simply as "single-issue" environmental protests.

In both our campaigns, we also find reflected some of the recent changes in the conception of ecological struggles. With regard to environmental associations, it has been observed that between the end of the 1990s and the beginning of the new millennium these have developed a more comprehensive critique of the model of development, which has made them link environmental concerns to the themes of global justice (Rootes 2005). With regard to citizens' committees, commentators have noted their "hybrid character, halfway between interest groups and social movements, oscillating between lobbying and participatory actions" (Sebastiani 2001: 111). A research project conducted in France came to the conclusion that "these movements are born from a conflict, and adapt to its rhythm. Conflict resolution can lead to them going into slumber or alternatively diversifying their interests" (Lascoumes 1994: 235). Local mobilisations are also spaces for the exercise of active citizenship; in fact, "their horizon is not always particularistic" (Bobbio 1999: 198), and they appeal to universal values (Williams and Matheny 1995: 183) while defending the quality of life within their community (Gould et al. 1996: 4). In our two cases, the interactions within a complex network of actors lead to the conceptualisation of a different model of development, defined in terms of "environmental justice" a combination of attention to the environment and concern for ethnic, social or gender discrimination (Schlosberg 2002), "ungrowth" (or "sober future" as quoted in the flyer) and "sustainable development".

In this sense, our campaigns can also be discussed in the light of earlier research on "growth machines", that is, formal and informal networks between public and private actors oriented towards increasing investment for economic growth (Logan and Molotch 1987; Stone 1993: 3). In both the United States and Europe, the crisis of the welfare state has accentuated the territorial competition for economic resources, above all private sources of investment (Thomas and Savitch 1991: 7). Politicians in elected office (looking for electoral support), local entrepreneurs (looking to increase their profits) and public bureaucrats (seeking to extend their autonomy) coalesce to attract economic investment in their territory (Elkin 1987: 36). These coalitions tend to become controlled by business elites in alliance with owners of houses and lands, bankers, shopkeepers, entrepreneurs, the local press and the professions. They often have the support of universities or cultural associations, as well as local politicians interested in the economic competitiveness of their territory (Le Galès 2003). Mobilised against these networks we find voluntary associations opposed to the reduction of welfare resources directed to marginal social groups, as well as resident associations who *see* themselves as damaged by projects for urban transformation, who propose instead a different model of development (Levine 1989).

One of the accusations against the growth machines is that they consider economic growth the primary objective, to which the environmental interest must be subordinated. Against this developmental view inherent in the growth machine model, local associations affirm the right to oppose projects they consider as damaging for their quality of life. In this perspective it should be underlined that the diverse interests within a given community make it hard to mobilise it in favour of its "value of use" of the territory, as against the economic interests that emphasise its "value of exchange". A comparative study of local conflicts in the United States has found that in general "citizen-workers find themselves locked out of processes, outmatched by other participants, and unable to gain legitimisation for their concerns" (Gould et al. 1996: 164).

In our two campaigns we *see* that the diverse social groups and political organisations that oppose large-scale public works elaborate (albeit at different speeds) a discourse on a model of alternative development, including not only defence of the environment, but also promoting work, health, justice and democratic participation. As cited in the flyer, at the centre of this mobilisation is "the question of democracy and justice in our country". The coalition for this "alternative development" gradually amplifies, involving new actors and developing new discourses. In contrast to the cases analysed by Gould and his collaborators, in our campaigns citizens become capable of conquering legitimacy for their own concerns, and are able to raise awareness in national public opinion.

From this point of view, we shall *see* that the capacity for mobilisation is linked to the amplification of the protest discourse beyond the defence of the environment, overcoming the local context and becoming linked to more global conflicts. However, we shall also *see* that mobilisation beyond local concerns requires some specific conditions, and is difficult to sustain in the long term. Not only do the national media pay only occasional attention to the protest, focusing usually on its more radical forms, but also the policy process only rarely opens up windows of opportunity (della Porta and Andretta 2002). The politicisation that comes with the shift from local to national (or even global) is not welcomed by all local participants. Sustaining a high level of mobilisation and public attention is only possible when local activists are able to link their claims to those mobilised in national and transnational waves of protest, but their own capacity to mobilise is also affected by the unavoidable ups and downs of the more general cycles of mobilisation. The shifting level of the targets and allies confront the protesters, as we shall see, with difficult dilemmas.

1.3. Resources and Mobilisation

If dissatisfaction is the motive for protest, this alone is insufficient to produce mobilisation. Research on social movements has revealed that collective mobilisation needs various types of resources. First, protest requires social capital, namely dense networks of associations that facilitate the creation of bonds of mutual trust between participants (for an overview *see* della Porta and Diani 2006: chaps. 5 and 6). The organisers of protest campaigns have to invest time and money to convince others, who are often discouraged to join or unused to forms of collective action. To protest efficiently they must also know how to organise activities that reinforce solidarity between participants, attract the attention of the general public and place pressure on the authorities. In both Val di Susa and the Messina Straits the success of the protest campaigns is linked to their capacity to involve diverse actors. Mayors and environmental associations, student organisations and social centres, religious communities and militant unions organise together into a network, which over the course of protest expanded to include different generations, social classes and ideological convictions. This rich tapestry of associations is partly inherited from earlier campaigns in defence of the environment: against the construction of a motorway and new electricity ducts in Val di Susa; against the transport of heavy goods in inhabited areas of the Straits. In part, it is constructed in the course of protest, with the meeting and cross-fertilisation between groups active on different issues (from work to counterculture), thus spreading beyond the local communities. Specific structures of coordination, flexible and networked, emerged in both contexts, together with norms and values that underline the importance of pluralistic mobilisation and tolerance of diversity (della Porta 2005a, b).

Within the resource mobilisation perspective, resources are considered as being given. Yet in our research we focus on how the protest actually creates additional resources. As we shall see, the meaning of the protest is constructed and reconstructed through cognitive conflicts on the conception of what is at stake. Collective mobilisation is linked to interpretative frames that focus on the role of individuals in locating, perceiving, identifying and labelling the events that occur in their life and more generally in the world at large, giving sense to their actions (Snow et al. 1986: 464). Frames permit the attribution of significance to distant phenomena, construct meaning, invent new forms of regulating relations between groups and find new ways to build consensus (della Porta and Diani 2006: chap. 3).

A particularly important element in the symbolic construction of conflict regards the identity of the challengers (Hunt et al. 1994). Previous research on territorial conflicts has underlined the attempts made to overcome the stigmatising Nimby syndrome: in order to stop new nuclear power stations, airports, incinerators or prisons, local groups try to overcome the Nimby label (Gordon and Jasper 1996: 159). The local committees that oppose an unwanted use of territory develop a rhetoric that distances them from accusations of particularism, shifting from a local to a more global discourse. Faced with those who accuse them of protesting for individual interest (rather than the common good) they develop a "not on planet Earth" (NOPE) discourse (Trom 1999). Often they define their protest through a procedural rhetoric that defends their action as opposition to the abuse of power and lack of transparency in public decision-making, as well as the collusive alliance between government and entrepreneurial interests (Gordon and Jasper 1996). Significantly, the flyer cited earlier argues that "what is defined as a particular interest ... is instead the expression of sovereignty of the population that inhabits the territory" recalling "a single struggle from north to south" (DME 17).

This symbolic construction not only has an instrumental dimension, but also reflects the very nature of the conflict. As Gamson (1988: 219) has observed, individuals act on the basis of a system of meaning, and the definition of themes, actors and events is a constant source of conflict. In fact, those who promote large-scale public works usually try to persuade residents to adopt the "value of exchange" paradigm, promising jobs and money, while those who oppose these projects are accused of wanting to destroy the local economy (Gould et al. 1996: 57, 115). To succeed in mobilising citizens, the protest actors need to build a shared vision of the community, as well as spreading the conviction that the resistance can succeed ("Stopping the Tav is possible" recite the banners in Val di Susa). In both Val di Susa and the Straits, the symbolic construction of community identity intertwines with the definition of interest among the diverse groups of the population, an interest that is increasingly less defined in material terms. The symbolic battle between promoters and opponents of these public works involves the ethical dimension of development, alongside the notion of public interest.

Another historical and environmental characteristic is important to understand the evolution of these protest campaigns: social movements are "networks of networks", and each node of the network is linked to another through multiple belonging of individuals and groups. Partly for this reason the protest intensifies at certain points, linking different types and forms of conflict. In our research we focus in particular on the transformation of local conflicts into global protests. Research on social movements has underlined the construction (during the cycles of protest) of social problems and collective identities that bridge symbols and interpretative frames from past movements with new ones. In our two cases, the conflicts over the Tav and the bridge intertwine with other conflicts and meet the broader movement for globalisation from below (della Porta et al. 2006). In this process, not only does the spectrum of supporters amplify beyond the valley and the Straits, but their schemes of reference become increasingly global. As the flyer suggests, the rejection of large-scale public works is linked to an alternative vision of the policies that affect the global level, reflecting the "commitment of those who want to slow down, who have begun to notice the signals of crisis in the planet" (DME 17).

Analysing the dynamics of collective action means going beyond a mere causal analysis by addressing more complex dynamics. If some political preconditions and collective resources influence the characteristics of protest, we shall focus our attention on the mechanisms that are put in place during the protest, denoting the emerging character of the protest campaigns (della Porta and Mosca 2007). We shall in fact reconstruct the processes of evolution in the two campaigns by looking at the capacity of events to interrupt or challenge existing structures.[2] We shall focus on the processes of cross-fertilisation in action, that is, the transformation of the actors involved in the protest networks that form during the course of mobilisation. We shall observe that protest campaigns and network structures produce a situation of intense interaction between different individuals and organisations. With the advance of collective action, above all in the peak of mobilisation, a process of cross-fertilization occurs which becomes reinforced thanks to the presence of multiple membership in various groups, as well as an intense process of networking (both formal and informal). This is visible above all in Val di Susa, where around the site occupations of 2005 we *see* the construction of discursive public arenas that facilitate the development of a collective identity, bridging the frames of different actors and creating bonds of trust (della Porta and Mosca 2007). The capacity to hold together these different elements is underlined by the No Tav activists. The slow process of cross-fertilisation is favoured by an intensification of communication and by interaction in the course of mobilisation. At the beginning, says an activist, "we stuck together mainly because we needed each other. The committees needed to understand what was happening and politicians wanted to know what could be done and with whom" (Margaira 2005: 138). However, in the course of action these alliances are strengthened through the development of common objectives and bonds of mutual trust: The success of the protest is made possible "thanks to the contribution of everyone who made enormous advances in reciprocal recognition" (ibid.: 39).

Here our comparative case studies will also reflect on the potential and limits of processes of cross-fertilisation in action. As we shall see, intense emotions strengthen the feelings of being part of a community. However, they are also difficult to sustain in the long term. If the memory of the harshest moments of the conflict is reflected in the mobilising narrative "it was like a fever" (Polletta 2006), they might be insufficient to overcome ideological and/or strategic divisions. The plurality of actors could intensify mutual understanding and reciprocal learning in some moments, but also facilitate fractionalism in others. Typically, highly emotional involvement might produce burnout effects and networking tends to be more difficult during the ebbs of mobilisation.

1.4. The Political Dimension of the Conflict

Whatever the interests at the root of a conflict, the mere presence of fear or injustice is normally insufficient to mobilise citizens. Research on social movements has suggested that in order for protest to occur it is necessary that those who are unhappy with a public decision *see* the possibility to shape its outcome through collective action. Protest tends to intensify not when there is greater closure towards the demands of citizens, but when channels of access to the authorities open (Tarrow 1994). The availability of institutional allies (normally left-wing parties), as well as divisions within the elite, represent opportunities for the mobilisation of new demands. Participation increases when windows of institutional opportunity open, particularly during the elaboration and implementation phase of the public policy decisions. If in Italy and elsewhere public decision-making pursues less visible public channels, there are some moments in which local institutions and public opinion are involved. Research on the construction of a high-speed rail link in the Tuscan Mugello has shown that protest intensifies when faced with divisions between and among decision-makers, public opinion and mass media (della Porta and Andretta 2002).

During the course of our two campaigns institutional allies emerged prevalently at local level: in Val di Susa, the local politicians and those of the Mountain Communities are an integral part of the protest; on both sides of the Straits the Mayors of Villa San Giovanni and Messina eventually took positions against the bridge (albeit with differing intensity and timings). Yet at the meso-level the regional governments of Piedmont and Sicily (respectively centre-left and centre-right) supported these public works, while at the national level a bipartisan alliance emerged in favour of what as defined as "strategic investment", between the centre-right government (and its supporting coalition of parties) and the larger parties on the centre-left opposition. Despite this collusion at national level, the protests actually increase with the acceleration of the decision-making process, given that this acceleration causes citizens to become more aware and involuntarily opens a "window of opportunity" for those mobilising against these projects. Acting in different ways (from marching in the street and to using procedural instruments and to placing political pressure), mayors and committees managed to intervene in the decision-making, utilising both institutional and non-institutional channels. The alliance between mayors and social movement organisations was, however, always subject to tensions and even crises.

Beyond the relative opening or closure of channels of access to public decision-making, the forms of protest are certainly conditioned by the characteristics of those actors and institutions that the protest wishes to influence. In this sense, the diffusion of local conflicts is linked to the transformation of political parties from mediators of consensus (intermediaries between the needs of the population and the government of the city, capable of forging collective identities) to political entrepreneurs that are increasingly media-driven and personalistic (Pizzorno 1996). In this situation, the complaints that were once addressed to local party branches now tend to become organised and presented outside parties (della Porta 2004a). In our two conflicts we *see* the weakening capacity of political parties to mediate between centre and periphery, noting instead the relevance of other collective actors, from associations to social movements. At the same time, faced with the weak mediating capacity of parties, the conflicts between centre and periphery become stronger. Local politicians playing their role as territorial representatives appear to be in open conflict with their own parties. These territorial conflicts become sharper in a reality of multi-level governance, where decisions taken at the national or European level appear to be imposed from above, thus reducing institutional legitimacy and the communication process between citizens and institutions. In this territorial hierarchy local governments feel that they lack political powers and are simply entrusted with implementing decisions taken elsewhere. At the same time, the resources of knowledge and legitimisation mobilised at local level do not find channels of access at the higher levels of decision-making.

The public decision-making process which produced the Tav and the bridge is seen by the opponents of these projects as a challenge to the autonomy of the local level in a decentralised political system. Particularly in Val di Susa (but also more recently in the Straits), the adherence to the protest of mayors from the main communes potentially affected by these large-scale public works testifies to the political-territorial dimension of these conflicts. In this sense, it signals the deep-rootedness of local politicians in their community, but also a weak capacity in mediating between the centre and the periphery. Moreover, in the course of the two campaigns the discourse on democracy actually extends beyond the notion of local democracy, traditionally understood as the delegation of policy competences from national to local level. The "sovereignty of inhabitants", cited in the flyer for a No Tav–No Bridge twinning, questions the very concept of representative democracy, seen as insufficient per se, while demands are formulated for a different kind of democracy based on the active participation of citizens. However, the challenge here is the capacity to empower local arenas, especially faced with an increasingly complex and opaque system of multi-level governance.

1.5. Our Research

Our research is designed around the binary comparison of two cases that have the common objective of mobilising against large-scale public works, and share a similar historical time frame, coinciding with the development of a movement for globalisation from below, to which our two protest campaigns are indeed linked. As with other protest campaigns, in both our cases at the centre of the conflict are decisions taken that regard the transport system. This theme is fundamental for the rights of citizens in general while raising particular concerns among social movement activists, who are aware of the effects of the communication system on democracy. The two cases differ, considerably, however, in terms of their context, both with regard to their social structure (industrial north of Val di Susa, economically "backward" south of the Straits) and their territorial characteristics (heavily urbanised area around the Straits, mountainous areas of Val di Susa); as well as their political traditions (strong leftist subculture in Val di Susa; weak traditions of associationalism and protest in the Straits). Even the structure of political alliances is different, with a national centre-left increasingly critical of the bridge (defined as "Berlusconian") but supportive of the Tav (initially proposed by a centre-left government), while the regional governments and provincial capitals of Piedmont (both centre-left and centre-right) are strongly supportive of the Tav.

As in "most different systems" research designs, the most interesting results concern the presence of similar paths and mechanisms, notwithstanding the environmental diversity. While never neglecting differences, a comparison of our two cases will aim in fact at highlighting common dynamics. Our analysis is in this sense not "variable-oriented", but aims at reflecting the complexity of our two cases (*see* della Porta 2008; della Porta and Keating 2008), discussing how context and agents interact through long processes.

Our reconstruction of these two cases is based on three principal sources. The first is the daily press, which chronicles the principal phases of the process and the public discourse of key actors.[3] Considering public discourse as highly relevant (if selective), we obtained from the press the official views of actors both favourable and opposed to the two works: their frames of reference, their symbols, their cultural claims. With regard to the protest actors on which this research is focused, we integrated an analysis of their discourse in the daily press (where it is very much limited and often distorted) with a systematic reading of their documents (flyers, petitions, press notices, manifestos, camera footage) obtained from the websites of organisations opposed to the Tav and the bridge. Beyond the literature of these organisations (designed primarily to stimulate mobilisation) we also wanted to *see* the ways in which public issues became intertwined with private relations, politics and daily life. We therefore gave "voice" to these activists through semi-structured interviews, integrating autobiographical material and public comments in books, websites and journals. Our methodological choice reflects a theoretical attention given to the subjective construction of meaning mentioned previously. The link between macro-processes of a social or political nature and their aggregative effects in terms of protest passes through a social construction of reality by those that mobilise.

In this sense our focus on the point of view of the activists is not a sign of partiality, but rather a necessary methodological choice in order to understand the meaning of their actions and being able to interpret them. The risk of simply reproducing the actors' discourse (not a banal result per se) is countered by the development of analytic categories whose heuristic capacity we test in our research. Explanation is here pursued as the understanding of the social construction of the external reality by our actors, not the singling out of a constant relation between variables – we would indeed aim at *Verstehen* not *Erklaeren*, at interpreting, that is, the actors' meanings (Pizzorno 2007).

2. Campaigns and Networks: Two Periodisations

In the course of our research we shall look not only at the dynamics of scale shift from local to global in our protest campaigns, but also at the reverse process (*see* Tarrow and McAdam 2005), with the related construction of shared meanings, common networks and multiple strategies. Using some basic concepts of social movement studies (frame bridging, mobilisation of resources, protest repertoires), we shall, however, aim at overcoming some shortcomings of a static analysis based upon the search of simple relations between causes and effects. In doing so we shall discuss the interpretative hypotheses hitherto presented: Nimby syndrome; transformation of the environmental movement; political opportunities and cycles of protest; cognitive mobilisation of resources for action.

Before undertaking such an analysis we should underline that networks, interpretative frames and repertoires of protests become transformed during the course of both protests. We shall now present a periodisation of each campaign, observing the phases that amplify and redefine the social base of the protest, and argue that such local conflicts go beyond the mobilisation of predefined interests, with the symbolic construction of what is at stake occurring through a process of aggregation beyond the initial actors, whose local or environmental frames become cross-fertilised with others in a network of protest that is increasingly inter-thematic and supra-local. This is what occurs in our two protests, with a progressive extension of the territorial and symbolic dimension of mobilisation.

2.1. The Protest Campaign in Val di Susa

The No Tav campaign has three phases (*see* Table 1.1). The protest begins with the emergence of information on the decision to build a high-speed rail network. The Committee promoting the high-speed Turin–Lyon rail link is founded in 1990 (presided over by Umberto Agnelli and the former President of the Piedmont region Bertrami), at the same time a Coordination of environmental associations begins to oppose this project. These associations are already mobilised in the valley against the construction of a motorway and electricity ducts (IVS 5). In 1991 there is the first picketing at a conference on the theme held at Susa organised by Confindustria,[4] Fiat, State Railways and the regional government. This begins a very long incubation period of the protest, with information initiatives launched by the Habitat group (founded by Legambiente,[5] WWF and Pro Natura[6]) where citizens of Val di Susa, environmental activists and counter-experts meet (IVS 5).

Other actors emerge alongside the environmental associations and committees, including the Piedmont Coldiretti (small farmers' association). Already in this phase the mobilisation from below finds support in local institutions, from the mayors to the President of the Mountainous Community of the lower Val di Susa, who in December 1995 form a Coordinating

Table 1.1: The No Tav Campaign

	Phase 1 1990–1999	Phase 2 2000–2004	Phase 3 2004–2006
Networks	Habitat (environmental associations) with support of local mayors	New actors enter the arena: citizens' committees, social centres and militant unions, association of farmers and social forum	Networks of interaction intensify with the participation of the population (not organised). Arci and Fiom also involved
Strategies and repertoires of action	Prevalence of informational and procedural actions, with some symbolic actions and the first street protests	Processions, boycotts and campsites	Non-violent direct actions including site occupations, as well as processions with growing participation and a general strike
Frames	Defence of territory, health, environment	Frame bridging with themes such as work, alternative development and global justice	Against large-scale public works and in favour of alternative development. Increasing emphasis on participatory democracy
Reach of action	Mainly in the valley, although some contact with French mayors and environmental associations	Extends to regional and national level with coordination of other No Tav actors	National level with increasingly transnational contacts
Institutional responses	Strategy of passive exclusion (no information, no involvement)	No recognition of protest, while making proposals for compensation	Militarisation of the valley and attempts at selective co-option

Committee of the communes affected by the project (Sasso 2002: 196). In addition to the numerous conferences and public assemblies, some of the most dramatic early actions are the reproduction in public of the sound produced by a high-speed train, and the giant No Tav banners placed on the mountains around the valley, while in 1997 the mayors unite in a national coordination against high-speed trains and picket the Ministry of Transport during a meeting between the State Railways and companies involved in the Tav project.

The protest is defined in this early phase principally as a defence of territory (alpine landscape and health of citizens), as well as the democratic rights of the local population to decide their own destiny. The right to information and participation is counterposed to an institutional strategy that is characterised by very little communication with citizens and local governments. In this phase the mobilisation remains focused on the high-speed trains, and on this theme some contacts are made outside the valley. Already in 1994, Habitat meets the High-Speed committees in Bologna, Florence, Bolzano and Novara (ibid.: 88) and in 1998 the Coordination of Italian Communes against High-Speed Trains meets (ibid.: 234). In addition, contacts are developed with French associations and institutions, a partnership established in the 1980s during the transnational protest against the electricity ducts in Moncenisio.

A second phase of the protest emerges from 2000 when the mobilisation increases, above all in the valley. Processions are organized in Bardonecchia (July) and in Bussoleno (December); in Turin and in French Chambéry (January 2001) against the Italian–French agreement to build a new rail link; at Avigliana (November 2001); again at Bussoleno (February 2002); at Pianezza (June 2002), between Borgone and Bussoleno (May 2003); at Chianocco and Venaria (winter 2003). Together with demonstrations that involve an increasingly large number of citizens, the direct actions begin, such as the occupation of the office of the Regional President Enzo Ghigho in November 2000; the irruption into the Regional Council in 2001; a blockade of the motorway and the gallery at Fréjus (March and October 2002 respectively); a blockage of the drilling sites at Pianezza (January 2003); the occupation of the building site of the firm AEM at Venaus (July 2003); a blockage of cars of technicians of the firm LTF (May 2004); as well as the countercultural activities (concerts, theatrical events, photographic displays) or actions to bear witness (such as the hunger strike in March 2001). In this phase there is an increasing involvement of the population of the valley: above all in the six-kilometre march between Borgone and Bussoleno, in which 20,000 people participate (31 May 2003), which becomes defined as "the first moment at which the people of the valley join the militants of the committees, activists and politicians" (Velleità Alternative 2006: 38). From 2003 even the least sympathetic press begins to note the capacity of the No Tav to mobilise the local community, or at least different social and political groups. At a three-hour march on 30 May 2003 (with a symbolic occupation of the roads and motorways at Bussoleno) among the 20,000 participants there are (according to the newspapers) priests and park wardens, fifty tractors of Coldiretti, local police who carry the symbols of the forty communes whose mayors are at the head of the procession, while the militant union Cub calls a strike in schools. The music of the village bands merges with that of the youth from the social centres and the banging of drums by the children of the primary schools (R 31/5/03). At the end of 2003, in the local pages of the national daily *La Repubblica* the No Tav are described as characterised by a "thousand voices": teachers, housewives, pensioners, workers. This image of transversal protest is present in successive events: the picketing of 30 October 2005 on the sites where the first works are due to begin is described by the same newspaper as resembling "an unlikely army composed of entire families, young and old" (R 1/11/05).

In addition, the type of associations involved becomes as diverse as the social base of the protest. As a journalist observes: "This movement, which at the start was isolated, from a certain point onwards gains new adherents ... who come from very diverse walks of life, cross-fertilising with the citizens committees and institutional actors" (IVS 6). First, the protests extend through networking and go beyond local or environmental actors. The protests at the Royal Palace in Turin (30 January 2000) are described by the press as "noisy" and "colourful", since they unite a wide range of actors. In addition to the twenty-seven mayors of the lower valley, present are the social centres, Coldiretti, Legambiente, Cobas (militant unions), Greens, Party of Refounded Communists (PRC), Party of Italian Communists (PdCI) and French activists from the Comité franco-italien face aux projects TGV. Alongside environmental associations and local political organisations the citizens' committees emerge as a new actor for mobilisation. The first is formed in Bussoleno (Velleità Alternative 2006). In the memories of one activist: "After the formation of the first Committee for the popular struggle in Bussoleno, spontaneous committees emerged in the towns of the valley, formed by citizens, politicians and activists" (IVS 1). Alongside committees focused on the issue of high-speed trains (Committee against the Tav at Venaus; No Tav Committee of Almesino), there are more politicised ones (such as the Committees against the G8 or Spinta dal Bass) (R 3/12/03). At the same time, the activism of the institutional Committee (mayors and leaders of the Mountainous Community) increases with the acceleration of decision-making on the Tav project.

The No Tav activities in the valley remain thematically focused for a long time on defending the local environment, but from 2000 links begin to develop with actors outside the valley. With the campsites (promoted by the social centres and the PRC in 2000 and repeated every July) links are established with other groups, particularly youth groups from Italy and abroad. Visible contacts emerge with the movement against globalisation. The No Tav committees participate in the demonstration against the G8 in Genoa (July 2001), and in the following year during the anniversary of those protests (held in Genoa) as well as at the European Social Forum in Florence (Velleità Alternative 2006: 16ff.). During the petition against the Tav organised in Val di Susa by Legambiente (significantly entitled "Why the Tav is not an improvement of services but a gigantic bluff of figures and false information"), one of the most prominent figures of the movement for an alternative globalisation is present, Father Alex Zanotelli, who has long been involved in actions of solidarity with the global South (R 3/11/02). Later on, Don Vitaliano della Sala (leader of the same movement) declares that "they cannot build these colossal projects on the backs of local people and in spite of the views of civil society and local institutions" (R 8/12/05). Furthermore, links are consolidated with movements in France against high-speed trains: transnational protests are held at Chambéry (January 2001) and Périgueux (November 2002), the latter during a summit between Berlusconi and Chirac. In September 2002 at the party of Radio Black Out against the Tav there are debates between committees of Val di Susa and French environmental associations (R 21/9/02) and in October 2002 around 200 protesters from the No Tav Committee block the tunnel at Fréjus while the same is done at the other end of the tunnel in Monte Bianco by French protesters opposed to the opening of the tunnel for big lorries (R 6/10/02). Particularly relevant in transnationalising the protest is a petition directed to the European Commission Transport Division in early 2003.

The enlargement of the groups involved in the protest also has the effect of extending the discourse of protest: from the candidature of an electoral list in the provincial elections 2004 (entitled "No Tav List: Defending the future") to the protests of mayors, political parties, social centres and No Tav Committees against the candidature of the far-right list "Fascism and Liberty" in these same elections (R 23/5/04, 31/5/04). Furthermore, defence of the environment becomes increasingly intertwined with the demand for "good jobs", the struggle against privatisation and the pursuit of social justice. In 2002 banners against high-speed trains are taken to solidarity marches of the Fiat workers, among whose 70,000 participants are many from Val di Susa, including representatives of the local institutions, unions, anti-smog associations, green activists and inhabitants of Val di Susa against high-speed trains (R 23/11/02). The intensification of protest follows the process of institutional decision-making: the Italian–French summit (January 2001); the first site tests and approval by the Piedmont region of the first building works (July 2003); the start of construction plans (January 2004); and the meeting of mayors with the commissar responsible for the project (November 2004). From 2001 the protest begins to focus its attention on the Objective Law (Law no. 443/01), which reduces the number of controls needed in order to accelerate the construction of large-scale infrastructural projects. While criticising this Law (approved by the centre-right national government), regional and national politicians continue to extol the merits of the Tav, offering only more dialogue and a substantial compensation package proposed by the regional government (R 22/7/03).

From 2005 onwards, with the decision by the authorities to undertake the first site tests in the valley despite the opposition of mayors and the Presidents of the Mountainous Communities of the lower and upper valley, a third phase emerges in the struggle that transcends the local dimension. When the terrain is requisitioned, the construction site built and the site tests publicly announced (by April 2005), then (in the words of one activist) "we realised that people were much more involved than before; there were not always the same people present … the people were angry, there was no way of stopping them, they began to occupy roads and highways: the people, that is, not the associations" (IVS 5). During the course of 2005 we *see* an intensification of protest activity and levels of participation: 30,000 march from Susa to Venaus (4 June); 15,000 demonstrate in Susa (5 November); 80,000 people in the 10 km procession from Bussoleno to Seghino (16 November); 40,000 people from Susa to Venaus (8 December); 50,000 people in Turin (17 December); and 10,000 demonstrators spend New Year's Eve in Venaus. This intensification of protest provokes the repressive reaction of the public authorities. As No Tav protesters occupy the sites where construction is due to start in Borgone, Bruzolo and Venaus (June) as well as in Seghino (October), towards the end of November the police charge at the No Tav protesters, clearing them by force from the site occupation at Venaus (6 December). On the other hand an initiative by the provincial and regional governments leads to political negotiations with local politicians. This results in the mayors being able to send a delegation to the intergovernmental commission responsible for the project (August 2005); the creation of a technical commission with the involvement of local politicians; negotiations for a moratorium on any works until after the Turin Winter Olympics; and the halting of construction until an environmental assessment is made of the project (December 2005) (R 12/2/05).

The opening of a "window of opportunity" within the decision-making procedure affecting the Tav leads to the protest extending across the valley. At the march from Susa to Venaus (3.5 km) held on 4 June 2005, over forty local mayors take part as well as environmental associations (Legambiente, WWF, Pro Natura, Italia Nostra[7]), school collectives, the Fiom-CGIL union, Arci,[8] Coldiretti, PRC, Greens, squatted social centres and anarchists, Social Forums and fifteen local priests (R 2/6/05, R 5/6/05). From mayors to activists of the squatted social centres and citizens' committees from other parts of Italy (e.g. Tuscan Mugello), all are present in early June during the site occupation against the boring of a 10 km long and 7 m wide tunnel that involves the communes of Borgone, Bruzolo and Venaus (R 31/10/05). It is through the site occupations (as well as the debates, meetings and social events) that the protest in Val di Susa becomes transformed into a more general struggle against large-scale public works, a transformation evident from the banners against high-speed trains out protests in the Tuscan Mugello and against the bridge on the Messina Straits (R 2/11/05). Above all, it is the violent intervention of the police that provides a national dimension to the protest in the valley. National press coverage of these events remains high between the end of November and the start of December 2005, a period characterised by what No Tav protesters have described as the "militarisation" of the valley with road blocks imposed by the police and the blockage of roads and railways by protesters. During the march held on 16 November 2005, "teachers, farmers, priests, bankers and students … assert that we are fighting for our way of life" and reoccupy the sites from which they were forced out by police. The 50,000 participants represent, according to a journalist, "a kind of Front of people opposed to large-scale public works from across Italy" (R 17/11/05). The nationwide general strike of 25 November 2005 also sees the participation of environmental associations, squatted social centres, mayors and unionists, priests and Coldiretti, and parties of different political leanings: "Northern League and Democrats of the Left, priests and anarchists: the faces of a movement without a leader" (R 26/11/05). On the No Tav website (www.notav.it) we read that in November "the confines of the valley have expanded and many groups from all over Italy participated". In fact, the month of November begins with a document signed by priests against the Tav and ends with a "white night" organised by Turinese students to protest simultaneously against the Tav and the restructuring of the school system proposed by centre-right government Minister Letizia Moratti.

The mayors and the Mountainous Community of the lower valley extend the repertoires of protest, both through procedural acts (such as the withdrawal of the delegation from the technical commission proposed by the government; the refusal to approve the agreements relating to the site tests; protests against the militarisation of the valley; threats to strictly enforce communal regulations regarding building sites) as well as through more disruptive acts: on 20 March 2005, the mayors of thirty-seven communes take their protest to Turin, holding their Communal Councils in the open on Piazza Castello; in June 2005 thirty mayors (wearing the national colours) convoke their Communal Councils in Venaus, thus preventing technicians from CMC from taking control of the terrain, while in the summer Communal Councils are held in the open during the site occupations.

In December the No Tav protest (according to the generally unsympathetic *La Repubblica*) spreads throughout Italy. On 7 December there is a picket against large-scale public works during the première of La Scala in Milan, with the participation of Nobel prize-winner Dario Fo. On 8 December while 30,000 people march from Susa to Venaus and block roads, motorways and railway lines; in Palermo there is a No Tav picket at the train station while in Naples the railway tracks are blocked ("No Tav, No incinerator, let's unite the struggles"); the Disobedients' social centres and "critical" unions protest outside the regional seat of the Rai[9] in Bologna; in Mestre there is an irruption into the offices of RTF and protests take place in Florence and Genoa (R 8/12/2005). At the same time, a No Tav Committee is formed in Turin with the participation of, among others, the Secretary of Fiom union, the militant union Cub and the Euro-critical parliamentarians Giulietto Chiesa and Vittorio Agnoletto (R 8/12/05). It is above all in the last two months of 2005 that protests of solidarity take place in Puglia (where the No Tav struggle is bridged with those against new motorways and regasification plants) and in Trieste (where the proposed Corridor 5 of the Tav will open out). The march in Turin (17 December) is attended by tens of thousands (around 50,000 people according to the organisers; 30,000 according to the police), while *La Repubblica* writes that "there is an increase in the participation in events organised by Italian movements, the many No campaigns: Sicilians against the bridge; the citizens of Acerra against incinerators; the No Tav Committees in the Tuscan Mugello" (R 18/12/05). The Olympic Torch Relay (for the Winter Olympic Games 2006 held in Turin) is contested by No Tav protesters in several Italian cities, and the headquarters of CMC (company entrusted with the digging works in Val di Susa) is occupied by protesters (R 19/12/05). After 17 December, when the President of the Mountainous Community affirms that the "protests have given us strength", the Regional President of Piedmont (Mercedes Bresso, Democrats of the Left) maintains that the No Tav "are weaker now because it has become a no-global struggle" (R 19/12/05).

The transnational dimension of protest strengthens towards the end of 2005. Though contacts with French committees involved in the Turin–Lyon tract are evident since the start of the campaign, it is the final stage of protest that becomes more explicitly transnational. The site occupation at Venaus will be visited by French mayors opposed to the Tav (R 29/11/05), who are also present in the march on 17 December 2005 (R 18/12/05). In January 2006 a large delegation from Val de Susa (5,000 people in sixty buses, organised by thirty committees in the valley) participate in a No Tav demonstration in Chambéry, France (R 7/1/06). Furthermore, the European Union becomes a site of protest, the reason being (in the words of one activist) "that, if Chiamparino, Bresso, Ghigo or Lunardi go to the European Parliament at regular intervals to obtain financing for the Tav, we should also go to Brussels as soon as possible" (Margaira 2005: 90). In February 2004, a delegation of politicians from Val di Susa participates in a session of the European Parliament, denouncing the violation of the European Environmental Directive (R 18/2/04). A delegation from the European Parliament comes to the valley during the site occupations. The Cardinal of Turin asks for dialogue and wants "the European Union to mediate *super partes*" (R 8/12/05). It is also between the end of 2005 and early 2006 when the No Tav struggle makes common cause with the No Bridge struggle, beginning with the aforementioned "twinning" between Rete No Ponte and Rete Meridionale Nuovo Municipio (DME 17, 29/12/05) and continuing with the participation of a Sicilian and a Calabrian delegation at Condove, Val di Susa, and at the public forum entitled "A Solidaristic Municipal Federalism, For Val di Susa, For a Sustainable Development, For the Defence and the Life of the Valley". The No Tav presence is strong during the national demonstration against the Bridge on the Messina Straits (22 January 2006), as evident in the coverage of local and national newspapers with titles such as: "Against the Bridge 10,000 march. Common cause with the No Tav protesters in Val di Susa" (R 23/1/06); "15,000 march against the Bridge and the Tav" (GaS 23/1/06); "In Messina the Bridge of No is born" (Si 23/1/06).

The acute phase of the conflict in November and December 2005 concludes with a partial victory of the Tav protesters, with a temporary suspension of the works and the start of a series of technical studies and negotiations. On 10 December a technical observatory is established for the Turin–Lyon line, beginning its work in March 2006. Its composition includes technical experts nominated by local politicians in the valley, the National Ministry, the Ltf (company entrusted with the building works) and from the relevant regional and provincial governments, with the objective of evaluating the need for a Tav (R 2/3/06; R 29/3/06). Its President, Mario Virano declares that the building sites will not open until the consultation period is over (R 18/3/06). The mayors also ask for a political round table, a decision that is delayed until after national elections (R 26/4/06). A commission of experts for Corridor 5 is nominated by the European Commission, and its final report is much debated, as it concludes that the risk of asbestos poisoning and soil erosion is limited, but the report is subsequently accused of being unreliable as it used material and statistics provided by Ltf (R 26/4/06). Meanwhile, a report of the European Parliament describes "an anomalous situation, highly damaging to the exercise of the right to freedom of movement of people and property" (R 26/1/06). A relevant theme (discussed also in the national press) is the financing of the works, given the problems in financing large-scale public works faced by the Italian government, which must co-finance the project with the European Commission.[10]

Alongside the technical discussion, a political solution to the Tav conflict remains uncertain. If the centre-left prevailingly opposed the Bridge on the Straits, it has maintained a wavering attitude with respect to the Tav in Val di Susa. The electoral programme of the centre-left coalition (Unione) in 2006 affirms the "priority of a transport and mobility policy and the integration of the national system with the European networks", but no specific mention is made of the Turin–Lyon line (R 13/2/06). The centre-left Prime Ministerial candidate Romano Prodi declared that Corridor 5 is part of the programme of the Unione while pledging to "discuss related problems with the affected population" (R 14/2/06), repeating a pledge he had made in a meeting with the mayors of Val di Susa during his preparation of the electoral programme. Since the victory of the centre-left Unione in the 2006 national elections, the new government has maintained an ambiguous position, tending to reiterate the crucial significance of high-speed trains and Corridor 5 while underlining the need to find an agreement with the people of the valley, even with an alternative project to the existing one such as strengthening the existing arteries of transport.[11] While the new Minister for the Environment, Alfonso Pecoraro Scanio (leader of the Green Party) maintains a critical attitude to the existing project, the Minister for Infrastructures, Antonio Di Pietro, declares himself to have no prejudices with regard to the Tav, while underlining the need to involve the local population in any decision (R 8/6/06), with the Prime Minister Romano Prodi confirming that the Turin–Lyon line is a strategic priority (R 22/6/06). When meeting local politicians in Val di Susa, Prodi promises to stick to the principles of "negotiation, discussion and awareness" (R 30/6/06) and to evaluate carefully the environmental impact of the project (R 30/6/06). Meanwhile the building site at Venaus is removed on 19 June 2006 and this is hailed as a victory by No Tav protesters (R 20/6/06).

2.2. The No Bridge Campaign

As with the No Tav campaign, the No Bridge (No Ponte) campaign has three principal phases (*see* Table 1.2). Already in the 1980s the Greens and Proletarian Democracy[12] had opposed the construction of a bridge on the Messina Straits, while in 1993 Legambiente contested the validity of the first Study of Environmental Impact proposed by the group Stretto di Messina spa (SdM).[13] Yet it is only in the second half of the 1990s that we *see* a campaign against the bridge that seeks to influence public opinion. In October 1997 during the first Prodi government (1996–98), the Superior Council in the Ministry of Public Works approves with some reservations the project proposed by SdM. This decision is supported by a local press campaign, including the daily *Gazzetta del Sud* (based in Messina), whose Director is also President of SdM. Between 1997 and 1998 the Committee between Scilla and Charybdis (Comitato tra Scilla e Cariddi)[14] is formed by intellectuals and professors opposed to the bridge, and is swiftly supported by the Greens, PRC and the main national environmental associations (Legambiente, WWF, Italia Nostra), as well as local associations. The Committee appeals to UNESCO for "wisdom to prevail" and asks that this UN body place the Straits of Messina under its environmental protection (DME 1). The real start of a protest campaign against the bridge does not occur until the late spring of 2002 with the mobilisation of citizens committees, social forums, squatted social centres, environmental associations and local political parties opposed to the bridge. This occurs a few months after the centre-right national government approves the "Objective Law" (December 2001), which defines the bridge as a "strategic" infrastructure. In May 2002 the citizens' committee La Nostra Citta di Messina (Our City of Messina) promotes a petition against the construction of the bridge (DME 2).

In the first week of July 2002, the Messina Social Forum (MSF) organises the first national campsite against the bridge, which culminates with a procession on the Sicilian side of the Straits. At the same time, with a joint organisation of the Calabrian Coordination against the Bridge and the Social Centre "Cartella" of Gallico (a small town close to Reggio Calabria), a series of symbolic and informational initiatives take place on the Calabrian side of the Straits. In the words of a Rete No Ponte activist, the origin of this mobilisation is closely tied to the movement for an alternative globalisation: "Four years ago we, a series of people almost all belonging to the Messina Social Forum, organised the first campsite against the bridge in Messina. From this initiative

Table 1.2: Phases of the No Bridge Campaign

	Phase 1 1997–2001	Phase 2 2002–2004	Phase 3 2004–2006
Networks	"between Scilla and Charybdis" Committee (intellectuals, local and national environmental associations, Greens, PRC)	New actors emerge: citizens' committees, social centres, social forum and militant unions. Coordinations developed and dissolved, some internal conflicts	New networks and their extension: Rete No Ponte; Rete Meridionale Nuovo Municipio; Coordinamento contro Grandi Opere. Now has support of local mayors
Strategies and repertoire of actions	Prevailingly informative. Appeal to UNESCO	Petitions, distributing information, symbolic and procedural initiatives, marches and campsites	Marches with growing participation from the population, symbolic and procedural initiatives, boycotts, twinning
Frames	Defence of the identity of the territory (landscape, environment, heritage)	Frame extension to themes including infrastructural modernisation, sustainable development and global justice	Against large-scale public works and in favour of an alternative development. Municipal Democracy
Reach of action	Prevailingly in the area of the Straits	Extends to meso-level (Movimento Meridionale), national level and even transnational level (European Social Forum, international campsites)	Local and national levels (No Tav, No Mose, No Rigassificatore)
Institutional responses	Strategy of passive exclusion (non-information, non-involvement)	Non-recognition of protest with acceleration of decision-making procedures	After initial acceleration of decision-making (2004–5) plans are blocked by the new centre-left national government (2006). Institutional reactions and (right-wing) countermovements in Sicily

we launched a message that was received by the Calabrians, who already had their coordination but subsequently made it more structured" (IME 4). We can hereby note that (more rapidly than in Val di Susa) the protests against the bridge extend beyond the local dimension of defending the environment. The presence of the MSF (itself a product of the Genoa Social Forum, which led the protest against the G8 in July 2001), together with involvement of the Greens, PRC and environmental associations, quickly gives a cross-issue significance to this protest, involving actors concerned with themes other than defence of the environment. Other significant steps are the participation of No Bridge activists and organisations in the European Social Forum (Florence, November 2002) and the proposal to hold an international campsite against the bridge (March 2003), presented by MSF, Calabrian Coordination and the Rete Sud Ribelle (Rebel Southern Network – RSR[15]). This is subsequently held along with two demonstrations on boats between Messina and Villa San Giovanni (a small commune close to Reggio Calabria), taking place on both sides of the Straits between the end of July and the beginning of August 2003 (DME 3, DME 6). Although only covered in the local press and *Il Manifesto*[16] (GaS, M, Si 24–25/7/03), the campsites are well attended. The No Bridge discourse thus extends beyond defence of the environment to demand the modernisation of infrastructure along eco-sustainable lines, stressing the "essential importance of publicly owned Water, Schools, Research and Health, valuing human, historical, anthropological and environmental resources through public policies that allow the socialisation and redistribution of income" (DME 3).

Beyond the social forum, environmental associations and political parties, local committees are also important here in mobilising initiatives (as with the No Tav protests), although they have different characteristics. Between Scilla and Charybdis is formed ad hoc in the struggle against the bridge (DME 1), while Our City of Messina existed beforehand and had campaigned on local environmental issues, such as local pollution (www.messinasenzaponte.it). As with the No Tav protests, the No Bridge protests *see* an interaction of experiences, organisations and initiatives: "Since we organised the first international campsite during the Messina Social Forum there was a decoupling of our forces, as different actors, associations, environmentalists and others mobilised against the bridge, and gradually began to intertwine" (IME 4). Even here, the mobilisation proceeds in parallel with the public decision-making process. In early 2003 SdM approves the new preliminary project for a single-frame bridge of 3,300 metres and commissions a new Study of Environmental Impact (SIA). The Calabrian Coordination, MSF and RSR respond with more frequent initiatives, including a boat procession between Villa San Giovanni and Messina, as well as the diffusion of "countervaluations" to the SIA conducted by environmental associations. In October the No Bridge actions are linked more generally to the campaign against large-scale public works, through the participation of Sicilian organisations and activists at the national demonstration in Verona (DME 5). As an activist confirms:

A link with the movement against large-scale public works is obvious from the moment in which we decide that we are not selfish and don't just want to save our territory, but that our struggle is the same as that of the No Tav, the struggle against incinerators, etc.; the problem is that the whole system that imposes these large-scale public works is outdated and must be reconsidered. (IME 4)

In 2004 the decision-making procedure accelerates along with the protest campaign. On 11 March the European Parliament approves an amendment that excludes the bridge from the thirty priority works for the Trans-European Network of Transport (TEN-T). While the centre-right Minister for Public Works Lunardi insists that the "building sites will open in 2005", Pecoraro Scanio (leader of the Greens) claims that the vote in Strasburg is a victory for the centre-left position and Massimo D'Alema (President of the Democrats of the Left) asserts that it is "a confirmation of the feeling that the project does not have a concrete foundation" (Me 13/03/04). However, the European Council of Ministers reintroduce the bridge as one of the priority works of TEN-T (R 13/3/04) while the European Parliament rejects on its second reading (21 April) the amendment it had approved in its first reading (11 March).

Parallel to this Europeanisation of decision-making, the protest campaign also shifts to the transnational level. From 17 to 25 July MSF organises in Torre Faro (close to Messina) the third "Meeting against the Bridge", with assemblies, debates and a series of seminars on diverse themes including fair trade, volunteering overseas, critical consumption, demilitarisation of Sicily, local democracy and participatory democracy, Mafia and large-scale public works and abolition of the CPT.[17] In the first week of August at Villa San Giovanni-Cannitello (on the Calabrian coast) there is the third campsite organised by the Southern Coordination against the Bridge, with assemblies, concerts and territorial initiatives, including surrounding the buildings proposed for demolition in the bridge project with red and white tape. On 6 August there is a demonstration in Messina and on the 7th one in Villa San Giovanni. Although the Commune of Messina had told shopkeepers to close for fear of violence, no such incidents are reported. The experience of the campsite (with the participation of around 1,000 people) is seen positively by the Coordination. The transnational dimension is also visible in the Straits, not only with the active presence of No Bridge in the European Social Forum (Florence 2002) but also in the international campsites organised in the summers of 2003 and 2004 with the participation of numerous activists from abroad.

The protest against the bridge moves beyond the symbolic and informational stage on 8 December 2004, when there is a National March in Messina. At this point it becomes a popular mobilisation involving many citizens from the area of the Straits and is reported in the national press (Ansa, Io, L, R, S 9/12/04). A kilometre-long procession sees the participation of 10,000 people, and includes political parties, environmental associations, social movement organisations and citizens' committees, as well as individual citizens; a coffin is carried with the words "With the Bridge, Messina is Dead". From that moment the protest is characterised, according to some activists, by a communitarian dimension, reflected in its "wide and transversal social base varying from upper-middle to middle-lower classes" (IME 3); in fact, the "social and generational base of the movement incorporates everyone, from nursery students to pensioners, from fishmongers to judges, teachers to students, shopkeepers to doctors. A heterogeneous movement that also spans right to left" (IME 1).

The mobilisation intensifies further in 2005, when the bidding process for a General Contractor takes place and the start of works is scheduled for 2006. On 12 March there are simultaneous demonstrations in Messina and Reggio Calabria, promoted by Legambiente, Italia Nostra and WWF, to protest against the yearly tax of 100 million euros that will be placed on rail tickets in order to pay for the bridge, under the terms of the Convention signed between the government and SdM (R 12/3/05; S 7/3/05). The various marches and sit-ins *see* thousands of participants; an enormous papiermâche-hen is carried to symbolise the construction of the bridge as a chicken that produces "a golden egg they want to exploit" (U 13/3/05). On 16 July there is a nautical demonstration organised by WWF (entitled "Wave after Wave, for the Straits and against the Bridge"): around 150 boats surround a feluca (traditional boat for catching swordfish), crossing the Straits from Cannitello (Calabria) to Torre Faro (Messina), points where the pylons of the bridge are proposed to be built. On 22–23 July in Torre Faro, alongside a demonstration organised by Rete No Ponte 2005, there is a "24–hour non-stop oratorical marathon against the Bridge on the Straits" organised by Legambiente, where representatives of associations, movements and citizens alternate without a break in asserting the reasons against the bridge. On 6 August over 8,000 people participate in the fourth National March against the Bridge in the streets of Messina city centre, organised by Rete No Ponte 2005 (Si 7/8/05). On this occasion, the political and environmental organisations underwrite a final document to launch a new initiative in the autumn and announce that they will occupy the building sites should these be set up (DME 13).

In the course of these protests, the reach of the actors involved is extended and temporary structures of coordination are established between them. On 5 June, a constitutive assembly forms the Rete No Ponte 2005, including among others Arci, Cobas, Between Scilla and Charybdis, Cub, Cartella Social Centre, Laboratorio contro il Ponte, Legambiente Sicily, Legambiente Villa San Giovanni, MSF, Movimento Nonviolento, PRC, Greens of Messina and Sud Antagonista. On 22 January 2006 in Messina, 20,000 people participate in a demonstration "to defend the Straits" called by Rete No Ponte. Beyond the presence of the main environmental associations (and their national leaders), this event sees the involvement of most national leaders of the centre-left coalition, the main social movement organisations, as well as citizens' committees, squatted social centres and other groups opposed to the bridge. Of note is the participation of the Mayors of Messina and Villa San Giovanni (both centre-left) and a 400–strong delegation from the No Tav Committee, the latter a result of the twinning process. This demonstration is well covered by local and national press and television news, all of which underline the varied political and social composition of the participants: the national daily *La Repubblica* notes that in addition to the political representatives there are also "environmentalists, families, mums with pushchairs, schoolchildren, scouts, all along the road from Piazza Cairoli to the Commune, as well as judges" (R 23/1/06); the local daily *La Sicilia* describes the "multicolour" features of the procession: "The yellow of Legambiente. The green of WWF. The red of the youth Left, but also the darker red of PdCI and PRC. And the red and black banners with an anarchic 'A'. Youth from the squatted social centres, environmentalists, boy scouts, children and parents" (Si 23/1/06).

In the ensuing months the twinning between the Ponte and Tav campaigns becomes consolidated and extended further to include other local mobilisations, which raise global issues (DME 27). On 11 February in Venice the No Bridge participate in an assembly of the Movement "No Mose–No Bridge–No Tav against large-scale public works" (www.terrelibere.org, 14/2/06), while between 16 and 18 February in Bussoleno a Forum is promoted by the No Tav Committees of Val di Susa, and on 29 April in Brindisi there is a demonstration against the construction of a regasification plant, with a new twinning between activists of Brindisi and those of the Straits (IME 7). In March, while No Bridge associations launch a boycott of the companies and banks involved in the bridge project (www.terrelibere.org, 14/3/06), the contract between SdM and Impregilo is signed, confirming the latter as General Contractor for the project (www.finanzaonline.com, 27/3/06).

After the national elections of April 2006 the ministers of the centre-left national government publicly express their opposition to the bridge: from the Minister of Transport Bianchi to the Minister of the Environment Pecoraro Scanio, the latter confirming that the state will revoke the contract given to Impregilo without paying any penalty (R, www.terrelibere.org, 18/5/06). Even the Minister of Infrastructure Di Pietro (usually in favour of large-scale public works) announces that the government will cancel non-priority public works including the bridge on the Straits (Reuters, 28/6/06), though its parliamentary group will vote against the dissolution of the society SdM proposed by the government (R 29/10/07). This change of heart from the new government was already announced in the electoral campaign, and provoked the hostile reaction of the local media in favour of the project, which launched a pro-bridge campaign (Si, 21/5/06; 15/6/06). The centre-right coalition in Sicily also formed a countermovement led by Raffaele Lombardo (Movement for Autonomy) with the participation of the main leaders of the Sicilian centre-right and thousands of people from outside the area of the Straits (Si, www.terrelibere.org, 6/6/06).

While neither protest campaign can be considered finished, their symbolic relevance in the geography of protest in Italy, as well as their duration and complexity, makes them extremely interesting cases to analyse in order to evaluate the dynamic evolution of conflicts between local and global dimensions. In the following chapters we shall elaborate on the processes mentioned here: from the formation of networks of protest, their actors and their functioning (Chapter 2), to the symbolic dimension of protest through an analysis of the discourse of different actors (Chapter 3), to an evolution in the repertoire of actions and their capacity to reproduce resources for mobilisation (Chapter 4).

Notes

1. Among others, Lindblom (1980: 123) has defined as appropriate processes "those which the citizens choose for themselves, no matter how stupidly".
2. The formative capacity of certain events has been described as "eventful temporality" (Sewell 1996).
3. If the press has often been used as the principal source for the most visible part of social movements (the protest) the information gathered has been accused of double distortion. Not only are the protests reported in the press only a small part of the overall protest activity, but the newspapers tend to focus almost exclusively on incidences of violence or large-scale mobilisation, or otherwise respond to momentary concerns in line with an issues cycle (McCarthy et al. 1996; Fillieule and Jimenez 2003). Our research on the press (including the local one) is, however, not oriented to a quantitative analysis of protest events, but rather seeks to reconstruct (through the integration of different sources) the different cycles of protest and the organisational strategies adopted.
4. Confindustria is the main Italian businessmen's association.
5. Legambiente is the largest and most important environmental association in Italy, with a moderate left-wing orientation.
6. Pro Natura is a federation of local environmental associations.
7. Italia Nostra is a moderate environmental association present at national level.
8. Arci is the main Italian cultural association with a moderate left-wing orientation.
9. Italian public broadcasting corporation.
10. The latter would cover 20% of the costs, around 1.5 billion euros of a 17 billion euro project according to the No Tav Committees (R 17/5/06, 12/6/06).
11. The proposal of an alternative route (supported by the Regional President of Piedmont) was firmly rejected by No Tav.
12. Proletarian Democracy was an Italian radical left-wing party founded in the mid-1970s that joined the PRC in 1991.
13. SdM was created in 1981 with the objective of finding solutions regarding the feasibility of the project. It was set up by IRI (its majority shareholder) as well as ANAS, State Railways and the Regions of Sicily and Calabria. IRI (Institution of

Industrial Reconstruction) was a state-owned company now privatised, as were ANAS and State Railways.

14. Scilla and Charybdis are the points of the Calabrian and Sicilian coast that define the area of the Straits of Messina. Their names refer to monsters that according to Greek myth guarded the passage of boats between the two sides of the Straits.

15. RSR was a network set up by radical left-wing groups and social centres in southern Italy.

16. Italian newspaper with a left-wing orientation.

17. CPT are the Centres for Temporary Residence, which enclose immigrants caught arriving illegally in Italy on the (mainly Sicilian) coasts.

Chapter 2

Networks and Cross-fertilisation: the Resources of the Protest

At first there were only a few of us writing about what was happening, holding assemblies and seminars explaining the danger the project represented for the valley. It remained at an elite level for a long time. Then the decision to build the high-speed link was taken ... this proved the turning point. Although there were still mobilisations in previous years, these were on a relatively smaller scale: a few years ago the demonstration in Sant'Ambrogio saw four to five thousand participate in a march, including the Coldiretti. The only party present from the beginning was the Refounded Communists, particularly in the valley, although the Greens later became involved; the Mountainous Community was involved too but there was no network between communes. At the same time information circulated, allowing people to develop an opposition to the high-speed link, sometimes even unconsciously. The turning point was in 2005 when the government had decided to begin the ground tests. (IVS 11)

1. Networks and Cross-fertilisation: an Introduction

The words of this activist underline a frequently mentioned problem for social movements, namely that the presence of a controversy does not transform automatically into collective action, particularly of a mass nature, as mobilisation of the discontented is required for this to happen. Mobilisation in both our protest campaigns is potentially very difficult, having to address complex technical questions and oppose the discourse of project promoters who promise economic advantages for the communities affected. In this chapter we shall *see* how these problems were confronted through a networked organisational structure, which expanded during the protest, adopting instruments of flexible coordination. We underline the wealth of resources that the different actors brought to the protest, as well as the tensions that a "multicolour" mobilisation of a "thousand voices" inevitably brings. In doing so we shall analyse the different advantages and challenges for the network during the distinct phases of a protest campaign. In particular, mobilisations that oppose specific public decisions during different steps of the public decision-making process may have a relevant impact on the opening (and closing) of windows of opportunity for protest (*see* also della Porta and Andretta 2002).

With regard to the organisational network, these conflicts went well beyond the mobilisation of predefined interests. In fact, the definition of what is at stake follows a process of aggregation that involves new actors in the protest, whose discourses become cross-fertilised with one another in a protest network that is increasingly cross-issue and supra-local. With regard to the mobilisation of resources, we observe the capacity of the protest to involve the local community, as well as to confront divisions (both geographical and political) within the movement (higher versus lower valleys of Val di Susa; Calabrian versus Sicilian coast; moderate versus more radical components). Crucial to the success of both these campaigns is overcoming the constraints imposed by the local context. The capacity to hold together different groups is considered a fundamental achievement by activists, as the process of mobilisation intertwines with the intensification of communication and the interaction between diverse actors in the course of the protest. This extends through a networked structure to the national and even transnational level, becoming part of a broader campaign against large-scale public works, linked to the development of an alternative global vision of development and justice.

The protest expands in particular when "policy windows" open, during the phases of acceleration in the public decision-making process, when the risks of the project being realised became more imminent. The extension of the networks of protest has a vertical and a generational dimension, with the adherence to the movement of diverse actors (local institutions and unions; environmental associations and squatted social centres), bringing about a reciprocal cross-fertilisation in the organisational forms, discourses and repertoires of collective action. If research on interest groups has underlined a growing functional differentiation (*see* Kitschelt 2003), this process is inverted in our cases because of the interaction of different types of organisation within a dense campaign network. While research on social movements in the 1990s observed their progressive institutionalisation (Kriesi 1996; della Porta 2003a), mobilisation in our protest campaigns is actually favoured by the participative organisational structures they adopt, which are better suited to gain the active involvement of protesters.

Beyond the description of actors and resources present in our two protest campaigns, our research seeks to stimulate a theoretical reflection on the characteristics and organisational dynamics of protest. Organisational structures capable of mobilising support and investing resources in action are crucial. If there is general agreement on the relevance of protest entrepreneurs, there are differing opinions on what constitutes the organisational formula most appropriate to sustain collective action: some praise well-structured organisations with substantial resources (McCarthy and Zald 1987; Gamson

1990) while others distrust them, seeing the process of bureaucratisation as limiting the disruptive capacities of protest by co-opting many of its actors (Piven and Cloward 1977; della Porta and Diani 2006: chap. 6). In fact, social movements tend to include different organisational models within a (more or less) dense and flexible network (Diani 1995).

Attention to social movement organisations has been at the core of the resource mobilisation approach, whose proponents stress that "the entrepreneurial mode of analysis includes both the rational-economic assumptions and formal organizational thrusts" (Zald and McCarthy 1987: 45). Social movement organisations must mobilise resources from the surrounding environment, whether directly (in the form of money) or by voluntary work, while they must also neutralise opponents and increase support from both the general public and the elite (McCarthy and Zald 1987: 19).

Beyond the instrumental function, social movements organisations are, however, also objects of identification for their constituencies, their opponents and the general public (della Porta and Diani 2006: 137). The different organisational forms present in our networks are not just functional due to the different environments in which they are active (e.g. unions in industrial relations, citizens' committees in territorial arenas, etc.), but also endowed with values nurtured in a long history.

In our research we view organisations not only as mobilisation agents, but also as spaces of deliberation and value construction. The first approach has been dominant in the social movement literature. As Clemens and Minkoff (2004: 156) have recently noted with respect to the development of a resource mobilisation perspective: "Attention to organization appeared antithetical to analysis of culture and interaction. As organizations were understood instrumentally, the cultural content of organizing and the meanings signalled by organizational forms were marginalized as topics for inquiry." In more recent approaches, social movements are seen instead as contexts for political conversation, characterised by specific etiquettes (Eliasoph 1998: 21).

This evolution reflects changes in the sociology of organisation, such as the shift from a closed system to an open system approach, and more recently the adoption of neo-institutional perspectives.[1] Our research shares some of this attention to the adaptation to environmental constraints and resources, but also to inherited values and path dependence. First of all, we consider organisations as socialising agents and norm producers that "do not just constrain options: they establish the very criteria by which people discover their preferences" (ibid.: 11). Organisations are therefore not just means for mobilisation, but also arenas for experimentation. We also share with the neo-institutional approach an attention to cognitive mechanisms (not simply mechanical adaptation), particularly to the ways in which "organization members discover their motives by acting" (ibid.: 19).[2] In our research we aim to combine an analysis of formal organisational roles with informal practices, general values and participation in protest campaigns. While considering environmental constraints as potentially important in shaping organisational behaviour, we believe that organisations play an important and active role in shaping their own environment. For social movements (as for other social actors) the organisation is not just a means but also an end in itself. The neo-institutional approach has similarly argued that "the relevance of relationships was no longer defined by the formal organization chart; forms of coordination grounded in personal networks as well as non authoritative projects of mobilization were made visible, as were influences that transgressed the official boundaries of an organization" (Clemens 2005: 356). In particular, individuals belonging to different organisations and groups interact during the protest actions, developing reciprocal knowledge and sometimes reciprocal trust.

As we shall show in this chapter, the network structure presents both advantages and challenges for mobilisation, as it must hold together diverse actors that are often in competition or disagreement with each other. The activists we interviewed stressed the importance and the difficulties of a process that aggregates diverse actors, such as the local institutions (section 2) and environmental associations (section 3) present at the start of the protest campaigns, together with the citizens' committees (section 4), social centres (section 5) and trade unions (section 6) that joined the protest later. Formal and informal structures therefore allow these diverse actors to become networked during both these campaigns (section 7).

2. The Role of Local Institutions

> There is an institutional committee that meets periodically, and keeps together the institutions and the movement; then there is the coordination of committees, with a movement dimension, and the meeting of Mayors, with a more institutional dimension. So there is a coordination of the institutions, one of the movement and a committee that bridges the two dimensions. (IVS 3)

This occurs in Val di Susa, where mobilisation requires the coordination of hundreds of collective actors and thousands of citizens. As this interviewee remembers, in our two conflicts even actors usually considered on "the opposing sides of the barricade" meet and coordinate their actions. If local politicians are often among the strongest supporters of economic development in their territory (Gould et al. 1996), research on local conflicts has revealed their occasional alliances with citizens' committees in protest campaigns, although their involvement is often temporary and instrumental (della Porta 2004b).

In Val di Susa, the centre-left coalition in power is divided along territorial lines. The Mayor of Torino (Chiamparino) and the Regional President of Piedmont (Mercedes Bresso), both belonging to the Democrats of the Left (Ds), are strong supporters of the high-speed rail project, while the mainly centre-left mayors and city councils of Val di Susa are strongly opposed. The alliance of protesters with the mayors is often cited in our interviews, with one activist recalling that "all the municipal governments and all the parties voted against the Tav in their city councils, both right and left" (IVS 3). In the alliance between local institutions and citizens there is both a division of roles and a reciprocal legitimation:

> It is evident that everyone has their own role and competences; there are things the institutions do and others that the movement carries out ... the aggregation of institutional activities and the push from the movement then become an unstoppable force: here in the valley the institutions have shown great courage, because, when mayors, provincial councillors and regional councillors act as shields between the police and the people, then there is a crisis of identity over who represents the state in that moment, and when there were acts of violence, or the spontaneous actions of the people in blocking roads and railways, even then the institutions were behind the people. (IVS3)

Of relevance to this mobilisation was the capacity of the local institutions to coordinate in a stable manner, overcoming not only their different positions (often linked to the extent that they would be affected by the construction project) but also their local party competition. Our interviews underline the coordinating function carried out by the Mountainous Community (uniting twenty-three communes in the lower valley). As the President of the Mountainous Community, Ferrentino (Ds), observes:

> We established a committee of coordination in the valley... composed of all the mayors, all the politicians elected in the territory (province, region, national parliament), as well as representatives from social groups (trade unions, Arci, WWF, Legambiente), each participating with at least one delegate. Though this structure was never formalised, its particularity consisted of the communal councils actually delegating some of their powers to this committee. (IVS8)

This process of coordination allows for the representation of subjects that is not necessarily by elected politicians. Difficulties emerge, however, when the size of the assemblies increases exponentially during the phases of high mobilisation. According to Ferrentino, the coordination open to the population has some "growth problem ... as after some time we no longer knew where to hold it, given that the core group was 120–130 ... while 1,500–2,000 people began to attend because they also wanted to be involved" (IVS 8).

The situation in the Straits is rather different given the sharp divisions among local politicians in their views on the construction of the bridge. The former municipal government of Messina and that presently in office in Reggio Calabria, the Regional President of Sicily (Totò Cuffaro) and the leader of the then Sicilian Movement for Autonomy (Raffaelethen Lombardo) are all affiliated to the centre-right coalition and strongly in favour of the bridge project. Yet even in the Straits there are local politicians opposed to the bridge, claiming to represent territories neglected by the state: the centre-left Mayor of Villa S. Giovanni (Rocco Cassone), in whose commune one of the pylons is due to be built, strongly opposed the construction of the bridge and even received threats from the Mafia in September 2004 (R 2/9/04); and the centre-left Mayor of Messina (Francantonio Genovese), elected in December 2005, also opposed the bridge. In the case of the latter this reflected an individual opinion (rather than that of the whole municipal government),[3] while the municipal government of Villa S. Giovanni expressed its "universal opposition to the bridge" and provided concrete assistance for the protest initiatives. The Mayor of Villa S. Giovanni underlines the importance of the logistical-material resources that local institutions can give to the protest: "The Commune of Villa helped out the young people, associations and movements that organised the international campsites in 2003–2004, giving them logistical, economic and technical resources. In fact, the municipal government was the sponsor of these two events" (DME 25, pp. 15–16). The offer of venues to hold meetings, human and material resources for protest is also very relevant in Val di Susa.

Although there is no coordination of local institutions in the area of the Straits, the role of the Southern Network for a New Municipalism (Rete Meridionale del Nuovo Municipio, RMNM) should be emphasised. This was born from an initiative of some Calabrian intellectuals and academics proposing to form a network with local politicians, associations and citizens from the Italian South, who showed principles such as participation from below, and the use of methods such as participatory budgeting, i.e. the process whereby citizens participate directly in the allocation of public resources. RMNM is in fact the southern node of a national network that "emerged in the European Social Forum in Florence, with participatory budgeting at its core, attempting to put together local politicians of the Left, associations and social centres that raise the problem of participation from below" (IME 6). From its birth this organisation, oriented to connecting local and global problems, has been particularly active in linking the conflict over the bridge with other conflicts, by promoting the twinning process with the No Tav committees.

Institutional actors bring important resources of legitimacy, logistics and coordination to the protest. However, there is a certain tension linked to what interviewees *see* as the different role of institutional actors, which leads them to more moderate solutions, with the concomitant risk that the movement will become "absorbed" by local institutions. In Val di Susa these difficulties were overcome thanks to the resources of trust that became activated during the course of the protest campaign. In the view of activists, it is precisely the presence of local institutional representatives in the streets that builds the trust between the activists and the people. As a militant from the squatted social centres recalls, "it was not always easy, there were moments of tension, heavy debates and clashes. However, when we were side by side, in moments such as the battle of Seghino on 31 October, with Ferrentino and other mayors regardless of their institutional function supporting what they affirmed publicly, then any ideological difference could be overcome" (IVS 1).

It is important to consider that the trust that grows in protest arenas can also be consumed while diverse actors interact in different arenas. Local politicians, given their institutional role, are in fact often called to represent their communities in intergovernmental bargaining tables, where they are pushed to play different games. If times of struggle strengthen protest identities, then times of negotiation push mayors towards compromises, which other actors often criticise strongly. Beyond the institutional arenas, local politicians are also involved in party politics, where their influence derives from a difficult balance between pressures within parties and (threats of) exiting.

3. The Role of Environmental Associations

> In the "Black Decalogue" environmentalists list ten reasons why the Bridge on the Messina Straits must not be realised: 1. It destroys a unique natural heritage. 2. It blocks one of the three most important migratory routes to Europe, the Bosphorus and Gibraltar. 3. It damages various marine species and fish stock. 4. The work proposed is larger than the one presented to the Environmental Impact Evaluation. 5. Millions of cubic metres of materials will be unearthed from digging. 6. Seismic risk. 7. Very few savings are made in terms of crossing times. 8. The building sites will consume a huge amount of water. 9. It requires hundreds of expropriations. 10. It is too expensive. (DME 12)

This document is signed by WWF, one of the largest and most influential transnational environmental associations. In the name of the environment, large-scale infrastructural projects are often opposed by environmental associations, which have previously mobilised against projects such as incinerators, high-speed trains and telephone masts (della Porta, Andretta 2002). In our two campaigns environmental associations again bring important resources, particularly in the early phases of mobilisation.

In Val di Susa, the protest against High-Speed Trains is presented as the continuation of earlier battles in defence of the environment that were conducted by national associations. As a Legambiente interviewee recalls: "If we look back to the early nineties, the idea was born in Val Susa of saving the river Dora Riparia ... it is since the end of the eighties that the motorway at Fréjus was being built and we were fighting so against it" (IVS 5). Although without success, these protest actors maintained their focus on environmental problems, perceiving their role as that of "monitoring, denouncing and exposing pollution in the Dora, above which the motorway passed and therefore ruined the river" (ibid.). The subsequent and successful campaign against electricity ducts in Val di Susa not only created networks of citizens concerned with environmental problems, but also represented a symbolically important moment in that "David was able to oppose Goliath" (ibid.), building cognitive and mobilisation resources that become reactivated in the actions against the Tav. Also in the area of the Straits, some of those opposed to the bridge remember their participation in the successful campaign against the carbon-driven power plant at Gioia Tauro (on the Calabrian coast), less than 50 km from where the bridge was due to be built (DME 20).

Earlier struggles represent an important process of learning, both when they end in victory (electricity ducts) and when they end in defeat (motorway): "If, at the end of the eighties and early nineties, the protests against the construction of the motorway were conducted by few people" (IVS 5), the coordination between environmental associations at the start of the Tav protest is seen as an important change. In fact, "Legambiente Val Susa, Pro Natura, WWF … founded together the Habitat Committee, because we understood that our three separate banners would make us easily characterised as the usual environmental associations that never want anything built. We used Habitat as a symbol to drag along others, then many people began to get involved" (IVS 5).

In the area of the Messina Straits environmental associations also play an important role, particularly in the incubating phase of the protest campaign: in 1993, Legambiente contests the validity of the first Environmental Impact Study (SIA) presented by the Straits of Messina group (SdM), and in 1998 participates alongside WWF and Italia Nostra in the formation of Between Scilla and Charybdis. Local environmental associations are involved after the first protests in 2002, which have a "drag effect on the parties and historical environmental associations" (IME 5) according to an independent journalist. In the first months of 2003 the national associations actively enter the protest campaign by developing and distributing "countervaluations" of the SIA.

In terms of mobilisation resources, the environmental associations bring technical-scientific skills, legitimacy in public opinion and strong informational and communicative capacities. As a WWF activist recalls: "In January 2003 we began to prepare our response to the Environmental Impact Study by the Straits of Messina together with thirty-two specialists of varying disciplines, then we disseminated our findings and even held public hearings in both Palermo and Messina" (IME 1). During the course of the campaign, environmental associations put in play their technical-juridical skills, pursuing various legal actions against the bridge project: recourse to the appeals court; denunciations to the public attorney's office; and appeals to the European Union highlighting the violation of Community directives on the environment (IME 1). The use of alternative knowledge is in fact rooted in the history of environmentalism, often nurtured more by alternative visions of the future developed within scientific circles, rather than by an opposition to modernity.

While recognised as performing important functions, environmental associations are sometimes seen as too "single-issue" by other actors. According to a journalist from Messina: "The established environmental associations have felt it necessary to distinguish themselves from others, and have been criticised for proposing unilateral initiatives" (IME 5). A source of internal tension in the No Bridge campaign is the perceived preference of environmental associations for allying with the better-structured and powerful organisations, regardless of their location on the political spectrum. In the words of a Calabrian activist from the "antagonist area", "the comrades of the movement are isolated so there is a proposal to include politicians from the centre-right in the battle against the bridge .... the proponents of this scheme (environmental associations and political parties) become the protagonists and open the movement to the right" (IME 7). While the phase of protest facilitates alliances between environmental associations and citizens' committees, the former tend to move more easily out of a specific campaign and focus on other issues and strategies. In non-protest arenas they accumulate resources (members, public funds, bargaining power) that restrain them from adopting a too conflictual attitude and behaviour in protest campaigns.

Other research projects have highlighted the possibility of incomprehension between environmental associations and other protest actors, in particular local citizens' committees (della Porta and Andretta 2002) and more radical environmental groups (Griggs and Howarth 2002). Environmental associations are often seen by the committees as part of an institutional game that tends to suffocate the activism from below of civil society, being too ready to engage in compromise, poorly rooted in the territory and involved in a structure of political representation that privileges strong interests and bureaucratised organisations (if not always collateral to political parties). Therefore the committees enter into tensions with these associations, that they see as counterposing "managers" to "protesters", "negotiation" to "conflict" (della Porta and Diani 2004). The local branches of the national and transnational environmental associations remain involved in the two campaigns, thanks to the strong commitment of their activists and the relationships of trust they build "in action" with other actors. However, they are often pressured by their national coordination towards moderation, as well as a preference for "winnable" battles that can be presented as an example for successful collective actions, consensus-oriented advocacy action and collaboration with institutions on specific, often symbolic, projects. The search for an equilibrium between local rootedness and global visions is often resolved in favour of the latter.

4. The Role of Citizens' Committees and the Organisation from Below

> We were five friends when we started to be involved in the struggles, all rooted in the territory – the thing we wanted most was not to extend the committee, but to build informal networks in the villages and to set up new committees similar to our own (which we were proud about), that is, to keep in touch with non-politicised people ... This has been our main task as a committee: to make the people aware and to stimulate them by setting up new committees. (IVS5)

The citizens' committees, as this interviewee states, emerged from below and spread above all in Val di Susa (but also in the Straits), becoming a crucial actor in the mobilisation of protest. Earlier research has shown that, especially since the 1980s, while environmental associations tend to institutionalise, protests on individual environmental issues are increasingly promoted by citizens' committees (della Porta and Diani 2004). Defined as organised, but loosely structured, committees are formed by local residents who meet on a territorial base and mainly use forms of protest to oppose (or request the improvement of) public works they believe would damage the quality of life on their territory (della Porta 2004a: 7). They are characterised by a flexible structure, limited material resources and a strong (even though discontinuous) capacity to mobilise protests (ibid.).

In Val di Susa, citizens' committees begin to form from 2000 "with objectives such as counter-information on the territory and opposing the first site tests" (IVS 10). With participative and flexible organisational structures, these committees tend to become rooted in a limited area, involving residents by appealing for an improvement in the quality of life, as well as symbolically claiming a territorial identity. By 2006 at least thirty such committees can be identified in the Valley (R 7/1/06). In the perception of activists, "the committees were one of the most important collective actors, possibly the most important until the site occupations. They emerged everywhere, searching for and gaining the role of popular protagonists" (Velleità Alternative 2006: 146).

In the committees there is a convergence of experiences and heterogeneous sensitivities, not only with an environmental focus. In the formation of citizens committees we *see* the re-emergence of citizen networks previously active in the territory. An activist from the Spinta dal Bass ("Push from Below") committee recalls:

> I became aware of the Tav situation many years ago. In March 1996 I was already present with my group, a cultural association that no longer exists... We organised cultural events, but already then the Tav issue concerned us a lot, so we decided to participate in the protest against the Tav with our banner. (IVS 4)

The committees spread across the territory through processes of learning rather than imitation. As one of its founders recalls, "after the formation of the first Committee for Popular Struggle at Bussoleno, spontaneous committees emerged in every town of the valley, formed spontaneously by citizens, politicians of the Valley, militants in organisations" (IVS 1), the first committees acting as promoters for committees elsewhere.

In the area of the Straits, citizens' committees pre-date the protest campaign itself, as they are already involved in issues that regard the urban landscape. "Our City of Messina" committee is created to confront the problems of heavy goods traffic unloading at the harbour and passing through the city (which causes not only pollution but several fatal accidents), and is one of the principal promoters of the No Bridge protest campaign. It is the initiatives of the citizens' committees, such as the petition against the bridge in 2002 (DME 2), that emphasise the relationship with "the people": "We are not claiming primogeniture, but before the street campaigns and mobilisation we had looked to carry out initiatives, first with petitions and stands in the street, trying to explain to people what would happen if they opened the building sites" (IME 3). Other forms of aggregation among citizens emerge during the protest campaign, always on the Sicilian coast of the Straits. Their "spontaneity" is stated in our interview with an activist from the social centres: "After the campsite of summer 2004, a spontaneous movement of citizens emerged at Torre Faro ... and on 10 September there was a protest of 1,500 people without any party labels, only No Bridge, anonymous citizens that went to the streets to express their opposition to the bridge" (IME 7). As Francesca Polletta (2006) has noted, in protest narratives the references to spontaneity maintain an ambivalent character, stressing at the same time a sense of autonomy from more institutionalised actors, as well as a legitimacy "from below". Especially in moments of eroding institutional legitimacy, this image can gain support for these "different" actors.

Faced with growing challenges to party politics (increased in Italy by the corruption scandals of the 1990s), the proliferation of committees is facilitated by their stress on mobilisation "from below", or, as underlined by our interviewee, "without party labels", as well as without "ideological environmentalism", a stereotype the press tends to mobilise with regard to environmental associations, but not with the more "popular" and "pragmatic" committees. The latter are seen to encourage "popular participation, people as protagonists, in an attempt to make the population of Val di Susa take charge of the struggle, actions, decisions, and the committees that emerge everywhere in the valley become a form of self-government, as in moments of decision, confrontation and debate" (IVS 1). As a journalist interviewee observed, also in Messina the committees are formed and rooted in the territory and hence become a symbolic reference for this: "Our City committee ... is an interesting case because their opposition to the bridge is born from the need to reappropriate a territory sacrificed into private hands" (IME5). While initially focused on this specific theme, with its very name recalling an ad hoc structure (Allasino 2004), aggregation within the committee brings about a thematic expansion that goes beyond the initial claims. As one activist recalls:

> I have been part of the movement since the beginning, from the Committee for the Popular Struggle at Bussoleno to the group "The possible Val Susa", to the Committee Bruzolo–San Giorio–Chianocco of the No Tav struggle ... within this committee part of the people tried to discuss not only the Tav but also other themes, water in the territory, participatory democracy and the ability to influence decisions. (IVS 9)

However, the relations of committees with other protest actors are not always harmonious. The committees, as an autonomous initiative of residents, are often greeted with suspicion by environmental associations, both for their territorial identity and for the protest forms they adopt. The very emergence of committees often derives from a schism within the environmental movement, seen by many radicals as being too moderate. They are also seen as more effective in reacting to decisions made than in promoting new projects. In fact our research illustrates that the "spontaneity" of their organisational structures facilitates short waves of mobilisation, and is particularly sensitive to the shifting involvements of short-time supporters, often normal residents who are not endowed with either strong ideological incentives or time resources. Other research has highlighted some of the weaknesses in the mobilisation of committees:

> The protests of committees proceed in an intermittent manner, in a reactive rather than a proactive capacity. Although able to create moments of solidarity and a sense of community, the lack of ideological glue makes it hard to hold the group together, above all in the subsiding phase of protest. An unequal availability of mobilisation resources, together with the media-driven personalisation of protest, favours the creation of individual leadership, despite the extension of participative decision-making. (della Porta 2004a: 26)

During our campaigns, it was in particular the radicalisation of the protest that kept the mobilisation capacity of the citizens' committees high, through the developments of strong communitarian narratives as well as feelings of injustice (*see* Chapter 4). Notwithstanding internal differences among citizens committees (between more moderate or more ideological actors), the steam of mobilization is the capacity to motivate residents by nurturing territorial types of identities (and interests). In the low ebb of the protest campaigns, however, citizens' committees tended to shrink and sometimes to disappear, although they tend to resurface with other names and making other territorial claims.

5. Squatted Social Centres

I am astonished at the way in which they have been accepted, and similarly the way they accepted others: you must not forget that they not only brought something, but they also learnt something, above all to discuss with people; when something must be decided, the "terrible" autonomists, anarchists or others, simply because they contributed to making a common decision will respect that decision. (IVS 2)

The people of Val di Susa learnt that we were not those the mass media and repressive bodies suggested we were: we were together in the site occupations, we looked into each other's eyes, and probably now they will believe less the criminalisation by the Minister of Interior and the mass media; they understood that we were neither crazy terrorists, nor warmongers, but guys and girls, men and women who care about this valley, its territory; who care about life – because Tav means death. (IVS 1)

The two quotations refer to the Askatasuna squatted social centres, recognised as a protagonist of the No Tav campaign. They underline a process of growing mutual knowledge, respect and trust that grows during the protest campaign, tested in action. Squatted social centres are similar to committees in that they adopt a decentralised and flexible organisational structure and are territorially rooted, but differ in their emphasis on the construction of counterculture (della Porta 1999) and in their more radical forms of direct action. These actors are typically present in local protest campaigns, such as the anti-nuclear campaigns (Rucht 1980, 1984). They are autonomous groups set up by left-wing radical activists (mainly students and unemployed youth) who occupy and self-manage unused buildings in Italy (based upon a conception of free spaces), where they organise political, social and cultural activities (della Porta et al. 2006: 250; Piazza 2007: 1); they contest the moderation and bureaucratisation of environmental associations and political parties, proposing direct action and participatory organisational models.

In the Val di Susa conflict, the squatted youth centres bring specific generational resources and competences to the organisation of direct actions, but they are also "uncomfortable" allies, often stigmatised in the press as being violent. However, the process of mobilisation in a common campaign has facilitated their integration into a protest network, allowing bonds of mutual trust to grow. In this respect, an environmental activist notes the presence in the valley of a political culture particularly open to various forms of resistance:

This libertarian component found itself at home in the valley, because we are a free valley, always against the current. Bussoleno had the first communist mayor in Italy; in this valley the resistance was born ... the greatest sabotage in all of occupied Europe. This libertarian component found expression because the people of the valley are free, combative, militant; but they also knew how to gain the sympathies of people, that is, the struggle managed also to purify them, those people Pisanu described as squatters, anarcho-insurrectionalists … all nonsense, they are excellent young people with an experience in the movement, who saw that the valley is a place where there is still a conscience, (IVS 5)

Also in the area of the Straits, social centres and their activists are important actors throughout the protest campaign against the bridge, providing political and organisational resources for the movement. On the Calabrian side the social centre Angelina Cartella in Gallico (a small village on the coast near Reggio Calabria) was one of the main promoters of the mobilisation against the bridge. It represented a point of aggregation and reference for the Calabrian Coordination against the Bridge; organised the Calabrian side of the joint initiatives during the 2002 campsite and the two campsites on the Calabrian coast in 2003 and 2004; participated in the European Social Forum held in Florence; helped to build the Southern Coordination against the Bridge. If the social centres on the Sicilian coast tend to have a shorter duration, many of the activists involved (mainly from the "antagonist area") are among the principal organisers of the first two campsites on the Sicilian coast (2002 and 2003), under the banner of the Messina Social Forum. They gave life to the Laboratory against the Bridge, one of the protagonists in the most recent phase of mobilisation; and promoted the Rete No Ponte 2005 ("No Bridge Network 2005"), which organised some big demonstrations in Messina (6/8/2005 and 22/1/2006), and pushed for a twinning pact with the No Tav campaign in Val di Susa (IME 4).

The squatted social centres are also important in linking local actions against large-scale infrastructure projects with actors involved in other themes and in other places, thanks to their coordinating abilities and the involvement in particular networks that they help bridging with the No Tav and No bridge campaigns. In the Straits:

On the back of the 2002 campsite, the social centre Cartella, which had convoked all the actors (PRC, PdCI, Legambiente, WWF, CGIL, Fiom-Cgil, Italia Nostra and some local associations), decides to retain the initiative and warns, in the assembly following the demonstration of July 2002, about the need to maintain attention, participation and information in the struggle against the bridge. (IME 7)

The social centres are often appreciated by other actors for their skills in particular repertoires, including counter-information and counterculture. This is a view shared in our interviews with respect to the social centre Askatasuna, whose activists "knew how to put themselves at the service of the territory, with intelligence and a spirit of sacrifice, without ever asking for anything. For us they are part of this valley. Even with the campsites, they had an important cultural function, while also playing an important logistical role, with great humility, never asking for anything" (IVS 10). Beyond the campsites, the social centres contributed to an innovation in the form of protest with "creative and lively" actions:

> There are other interesting struggles now such as that against the precariousness of work for the young. Through the Laboratory against the Bridge, young people came from the Messina Social Forum and the squatted social centres and in their struggle against the bridge found the possibility to aggregate. We are talking about this creative and lively component that innovated in the No Bridge movement, which was perhaps a bit too rigid. (IME 5)

Nevertheless, there was no lack of tensions and difficulties in building alliances between actors with diverse conceptions of the movement and of participation. During the No Bridge campaign, on the one hand the political management and organisation of the coordinations and campsites increased the role and influence of the Cartella social centre on the Calabrian side; yet on the other hand it also produced wearing out outcomes and internal and external conflictual dynamics that led to numerous splits and "recompositions", with the exit of the older and more politicised component from the social centre and the end of the involvement of Cartella in the No Bridge campaign. As mentioned in the narration of a Calabrian militant, "the social centre activists perceived their commitment in the No Bridge initiatives as disproportionate to that of other groups and, even if the outcome was very positive with a high participation, they felt themselves alone in organising and managing the campsite" (IME 7). Therefore, despite the success of the initiatives, tensions developed both between Cartella and the moderate components of the movements (parties and environmental associations) and within the social centre: "the younger comrades of the Cartella get angry with the older ones, accusing them of having used them as simple 'labourers', and not being given the political responsibility they feel they deserve for their work and their commitment" (IME 7).

Again in this case, the tensions were often (at least temporarily) resolved through common actions. As an interviewee from Val di Susa notes with respect to Askatasuna, "they were present in the most difficult moments, so they not only were welcomed but proved a fundamental element of the struggle, which held us together because we think that the struggle must begin from below" (IVS 10). Reciprocal learning and growing trust cannot, however, eliminate differences in the visions and practices of social centres and other actors, with potential divisions (or at least diminishing interactions) during the lulls of mobilisation.

6. Trade Unions and Workers

> The removal of the railway node involved closing some stations and abolishing discounts for students and workers. Railway tickets began to cost more and the services began to get poorer – because the maintenance of the locomotives, previously made every so many kilometres in order to guarantee safety on the job, was no longer done. The privatisation of the railway was the reason for our protest, but also the Tav; so our struggle was and is against the waste of public money for useless works, and for a real possibility of movement for people … we do not want this valley to be the starting point of a corridor without life and we do not want other places in Italy and in the world to become territories where great business and global market goods go through, but where people cannot live anymore. (IVS 10)

This quotation from an interview with a PRC activist underlines the role of labour issues in territorial conflicts. Trade unions are normally very reluctant actors to involve in local conflicts, particularly regarding economic projects that give the hope of an increase in employment. The Piedmont secretary of the main Italian union, CGIL, on the occasion of a strike in the valley called against the Tav, argued that "the tensions in Val di Susa, unfortunately … risk distancing that place from the general interest" (R 5/11/05). A similar position has been adopted by the other large union, CISL, whose meeting held at the building sites of Bruzolo is heavily contested by No Tav activists (R 27/3/06). Also, in the area of the Straits (particularly in Messina), CISL and UIL (Italy's third main union) declare themselves to be favourable to the construction of a bridge, considering it to be a project that would create employment. The General Secretary of UIL is defined as "one of the strongest remaining supporters of the bridge" (IME 5). In contrast CGIL, despite its radical wing being opposed to the project, is accused by activists interviewed of maintaining an ambiguous position.

In both our cases the positions of the main unions are, however, contrasted by a consistent participation of workers and their representatives in the protest campaigns. In Val di Susa, the struggle against high-speed trains takes place in an environment with strong working class traditions (or, at least, their strong myth; *see* Chapter 3), intertwining with the mobilisation of railway workers against privatisation. As an interviewee recalls:

> Our struggle occurred at the same time as one in favour of defending public railways and the railway centre at Bussoleno … which was very important; it gave work to lots of people and was an important place of socialisation: the Necci Plan proposed its closure, because it foresaw the privatisation of the public railways; at the same time they were discussing the Tav, strengthening at least 5,000 km of line compatible with high-speed out of a total 16,000 km. (IVS 10)

In a similar manner, the struggle of railway workers in Messina to maintain their levels of occupation and improve safety at work became intertwined with the campaign against the bridge. According to an interviewee:

An important role was recently played by some militant unions representing workers with flexible contracts, who linked the question of the bridge to their situation at work. The State Railways has been trying for years to eliminate the node at the Straits, substituting this with private ferry companies. This made it possible for such a sector, which is fighting for jobs and security at work, to identify in the bridge issue one of their struggles. (IME 6)

One of the links between workers and the protest against large-scale infrastructural projects is the defence of public health, a theme to which some unions are particularly sensitive. For example, a critical unionist recalls that:

The question of social harm is one of the key issues addressed by Cub (Unitary Confederation from the Base): from the petrochemicals of Porto Marghera to the demonstrations in Acerra, Scanzano ... Cub has always been in favour of movements that oppose socially harmful projects ... we have a certain idea of society and the rights of workers within it that has seen the collaboration of doctors, university researchers, industrial workers and collectives on issues regarding quality of life. (IVS 2)

In Messina too, the militant unions (above all Cub and Cobas) were from the start against the bridge: "The organisations from the base, Cub, Cobas, which are quite strong here, have always been protagonists in the struggle" (IME 6). In particular, the Cub of Messina already in June 2002 declared that: "The Bridge is not necessary for work ... for transport ... for the environment ... Let's fight for: water in all Sicilian houses, the completion of the unfinished motorways, the relaunch and modernisation of the railways, transport via sea and plane, the recovery of our environmental and cultural assets, in order to sustain a discerning and not destructive tourism" (DME 26).

The protest campaigns have the effect of raising awareness among members of the confederal unions as well, with a "push from below" occurring within these organisations. In Val di Susa, the protests against the Tav saw the participation of FIOM, which, in the words of an interviewee, enters "with determination and decision. It was good because at an assembly in Bussoleno many workers asked their unions to demand a general strike in the valley" (IVS 6). In this respect, some talk of a generational transformation, recalling that: "The No global movement has had an effect on some FIOM activists, those that entered the factories after 1980" (Velleità Alternative 2006: 92). Even on the

Straits, CGIL decided (despite some uncertainty) "to actively participate in the last demonstration (August 2005) and thus declared itself against the bridge, even with its own distinct concerns over the project" (IME 4). With regard to this "re-appropriation from below", it should be noted that "within CGIL there were already elements that pushed for a clear and coherent position against the bridge" (IME 5). In fact, according to an interviewee:

> The unions have always been in favour of the bridge. Today they pretend not to have been. CISL was the most openly in favour of the idea of a bridge. CGIL has always had two opposing positions, one close to the Ds and hence to the cooperatives that would compete for projects related to the bridge, while the other is broadly against the project. And UIL is in favour. (IME 3)

In the demonstrations of Val di Susa, workers and their representatives join many priests that represent their local parishes. In this respect, an environmental activist remembers that:

> A historical group that helped develop the "Dialogue in the Valley" was a newspaper founded in the early seventies by a priest from Condove and a self-taught worker, which led to the first initiative in a European factory against the production of weapons ... through Christian socialism the priests of the mountains and the valleys were always alongside the movement, as they were concerned with the problems of their people and would not accept any diktat. (IVS 5)

While displaying some of the contradictions with regard to the traditional faith in progress that has motivated the workers' movement, the participation of unions and workers brings to these protest campaigns both legitimacy and capacity for mobilisation. In addition, they enrich the discourse with references to a "good job" and attention to public services, which contributes to the creation of symbolic, supra-local frames that are not exclusively environmental in their protest against large-scale public works. Here also the consolidation of the union positions in the protest networks is contingent upon the strengths and weaknesses of the labour organisations, and the cyclical evolution of labour struggles. While the more radical critical unions in fact have a fragmented presence (with a strong capacity to promote short and/or localised waves of protest), the national unions' attitudes in Italy are still very much influenced by the colour of the national governments, with more conflictual attitudes when the right is in power, and more moderate tones when the centre-left is. In both types of unions, even in a traditionally politicised labour environment, issues not directly related to working and salary conditions spread less easily from the most active unionists to simple members (della Porta 2006).

7. Deciding in the Network

> It is clear that in the coalition there are different positions, but the same applies to the movement and nevertheless we agreed splendidly, on the basis of the idea that we build a path together, then everyone makes the proper actions in their respective contexts, and in this way the repertoire of actions expands. (IVS 8)
>
> One says: "I'd like to make this happen, help me", and because we know it is better that more things are done, in order to be covered by the media, to extend the front, to make the politicians aware that we don't want the bridge, the adherence is spontaneous; it never happens that someone says: "no, I won't join." (IME 1)

Until here we have stressed a plurality within the two campaigns that grows with the expansion of the network, bringing new material and symbolic resources while increasing potential tensions. In fact, these diverse actors interact within a networked structure, both dense and complex, which took different characteristics in Val di Susa and in the area of the Straits. We have, however, also stressed cleavages and tensions, which are more likely to manifest themselves during the low ebbs of mobilisation.

In the No Tav campaign, a networked model allows for an extensive participation. The "push from below" is evident in the search for different forms of democracy within the internal structure of the movement, with a particular emphasis on participation. In the words of an interviewee, "for some time the inhabitants of Val di Susa stopped delegating every type of decision, even to the same local politicians that supported us in the struggle. There is a desire to become protagonists, so the assemblies were crowded with many interventions by inhabitants that wanted to have their say and to participate" (IVS 1). Even the organisations of the movement are less capable of controlling their activists: while in the 1970s and 1980s the widespread image is that "everyone mobilised behind their own party or group and brought a certain number of people to the streets, today people take to the streets regardless" (Velleità Alternative 2006: 94). In both Val di Susa and the Messina Straits, the process mobilisation is described as creating a "political laboratory", which suggests an arena open to all in which anyone can discuss its concerns and make its proposals, with reciprocal influence taking place between different actors: "The increasingly lively mix between even very different components … this ability to cross-fertilise and put aside initial distrust, identifying a common objective to attain, produces an example of a political laboratory, an experiment of different forms of participation where decisions are taken with the consensus and approval of everyone" (IVS 6).

Decision-making is presented here as deliberative, that is, based on convincing others through reason and argument. As an interviewee from Val di Susa notes:

One of the good things is that none of the different groups abused the other, there was mutual respect. We speak in unison against the Tav, but the avenues to arrive at this decision are different and complementary … our strength is the reason contained in the arguments we bring. We develop a general reasoning (not just mine or yours), but in the Greek sense logos, which bridges the diverse arguments and not in a partisan manner. (IVS 5)

The capacity to "attempt synthesis" is linked to the growing trust in a context of reciprocal recognition (IVS 2). Thus divergences are perceived by the activists as conditions that actually enrich the movement if these take the form of discussions in open assemblies with diverse opinions that people are willing to take into consideration. In this way, differences are seen as "physiological, especially for a heterogeneous movement like ours, including politicians, activists, normal people" (IVS 7). The exchange of arguments is seen as a basis for creating consensus, given that (according to one interviewee) "there is a search for unanimity; if there is no consensus then things are not done. It is interesting to observe this capacity for interaction between actors that would normally never look at one another" (IVS 6).

In Val di Susa, the search for consensus is seen as a fundamental aim of the formal coordination of the protest campaign. The coordination of mayors in the communes affected by the project consisted of around forty communes and the Mountainous Community. The President of the latter, Ferrentino (DS), observes with regard to the coordination:

It functions in a very flexible way: the president arrives, discusses the issues that have come up since the last meeting, in order to inform and to make proposals for the future. Then we discuss for hours, argue, eventually find a solution, at least so far it has gone like this, we have found shared solutions … we have never had to hold a vote since the participation broadened. (IVS 8)

Even in the institutional conferences, where politicians, committees, associations and social centres meet, the decision-making method is seen as consensual: "We've never held a vote, for in an excess of democracy everyone had their say … after hours of discussion, which focused on specific points, we reached a shared conclusion, a point of agreement that could never be total; yet it was never necessary to hold a vote" (IVS 7). In a similar manner, discussion is privileged also by the coordination of committees, which adopts an assembly structure. According to an interviewee, "the committees have a coordination where they discuss, hear each other's views and confront their opinions. Decisions are always taken collectively in large assemblies, naturally respecting the right to dissent within the assembly" (IVS 10). An idea diffused among activists is that within the movement "in reality nobody decides, there are some people better prepared and more recognisable than others, but everybody's view is discussed, according to the circumstances. This is democracy from below, participative" (IVS 11).

Our interviewees often underline the relevance of mobilisation in common collective actions as a process creating reciprocal trust and allowing a fundamentally consensual style of decision-making to emerge: "Here what you say matters, but what matters most is what you do and how you do it: the population never theorised the problem of how to take decisions and act; action is the fundamental element here, based on the context, on the situation. The forms to decide are then found spontaneously, in order to decide, meet, act, think" (IVS 1). While forms of assembly often have their faults, particularly in terms of delaying decisions, they also possess "richness" in terms of their capacity to construct shared identities. As an interviewee recalls:

> We are a varied movement, for whom taking a decision is not easy ... there are no rules for discussion and this is a richness that poses some constraints, as we were never able to establish a "crisis unit", while many initiatives are unconnected, even though they subsequently converge on a single objective ... let's say we are in an open sea and this is both our strength and our constraint. (IVS 11)

The necessity but also the difficulties of becoming networked are underlined in the area of the Straits, where the organisational structure and internal decision-making procedures only partially resemble those in Val di Susa. First, there is a greater differentiation of roles between, on the one hand, activists who promote and manage initiatives and the structures of coordination, and, on the other, citizens limiting themselves to participating in the protest. In the views of one interviewee: "The difference with Val di Susa is notable. There is a No Bridge population here also, but one that delegates decisions, that wants to participate in initiatives but not in the organisational stages" (IME 6). If even here the networked structure of the protest is evident in the creation of various coordinations, the decision-making process does not seem to follow a consensual assembly structure, but to take the form instead of discussion between small nuclei of activists (almost always belonging to groups or organisations) who promote various initiatives, to which other activists or groups adhere to individually or as representatives of other organisations. This is defined by one interviewee as an informal mechanism: "It is not the consensual method ... while sometimes one or more actors, usually after a national push, formally adhere to joint initiatives, they may also participate in a personal manner without the formal adherence of the referring organisation" (IME 5).

The protest campaign in the area of the Straits is less popular than in Val di Susa, so as a result the coordination process remains weaker and more informal, with alliances only on specific initiatives and greater difficulty in establishing a coherent network. In fact, the different coordinations and networks that succeed each other chronologically often change names and form ad hoc around specific initiatives:

> Often through an event a coordination is created: at the 2002 campsite the battle against the bridge was led by the social forum movement on the initiative of the Messina Social Forum; another example is Rete No Ponte which was constituted in view of the demonstration on 22 January 2006 … from a formal point of view, the structures that were formed for an event were coordinations and networks of political organisations, environmentalists, committees, etc. (IME5)

Consensus is created with more intermittent and informal modalities than in Val di Susa. In the words of an interviewee: "There are some things that are chosen at a moment in time because they seem appropriate. There is a coordination of different initiatives that occasionally tries to create broader initiatives. Yet there are no formal organs, despite a substantive and clear decisional network" (IME 2).

Continuity in the movement (especially in Messina) is linked to the consolidation of interactions between restricted nuclei of activists, re-mobilising in different campaigns on individual initiatives and "maintaining a historical memory from 2002 till now. These individuals were the engine of the protest and promoted several initiatives bringing behind them their organisation … these nuclei of activists moved on their own initiative, building relations, having an impact on mass media, on the networks, able to catalyse the process of mobilisation" (IME 5). In this sense, the short life of the coordinating structures can be attributed to the "internal dynamics often created by personal relations, leadership problems", seen as negative for the divisions they may cause, but also capable of exercising a "positive dragging function over their respective organisations" (IME 5). The dynamics of collaboration on the one hand and the dynamics of competition and conflict on the other in turn reflect the geographical divisions (Sicilian versus Calabrian coast) and political-ideological differences (moderate versus radical) existing within the movement.

Despite these evident internal differences the No Bridge campaign also witnessed an increase in mobilisation, both in terms of participation in mass initiatives and in the extension of networks beyond the area of the Straits. As in Val di Susa, the territorial up-ward scale shift in the campaign helps to resolve internal tensions. For example, in the demonstration on 22 January 2006:

> there were problems between the different elements of the movement, because not everyone agreed in the beginning to the twinning No Tav–No Bridge; some did not want to leave the local ambit, the more moderate side had problems because some of the centre-left is in favour of the Tav … events eventually forced their hand, the No Tav mobilised

and came down here with 300 people, well visible at the front of the march. (IME 6)

The impression conveyed by the activists is that "in our dialogue we managed to find unity, despite some frictions and antagonisms, perhaps inevitable in any movement" (IME 6). Even in the Straits, some innovations can be seen in the functioning of the new citizens' coordination, which "recognised the different modalities and intertwining paths of the struggle, without stopping any. The modality adopted by Rete No Ponte 2005 was that of making the biggest decisions in a collegial manner, appealing to all the groups that cooperate within this movement, with each group then taking an individual path in order to reach this conclusion" (IME 4).

8. Concluding Remarks

In our two protest campaigns mobilisation is produced by multiple and (both socially and ideologically) heterogeneous actors. These become "networked in action" with different modalities in Val di Susa and the Messina Straits; yet in both cases they extend vertically from above (activists) to below (citizens), as well as along the generational dimension (young and old). The different protest organisations not only perform instrumental functions, but also bring specific strategies and norms to the protest that are not exclusively evaluated on their effectiveness. As we observed in other chapters of this volume (*see* also della Porta and Piazza 2007), these different organisations contribute specific repertoires of action and frames of reference, derived from their traditional organisational features, becoming reciprocally cross-fertilised during the course of the campaign. For social movements (as with other social actors) the organisation is a means but also an end in itself. Each actor contributes resources for mobilisation, together with specific norms and visions of the world. It is during the campaign that resources become mobilised and transformed "in action" and tensions are overcome (della Porta and Mosca 2007).

A difference here with respect to many other territorial conflicts is that local institutions (above all but not exclusively in Val di Susa) are part of the protest front from the very beginning, bringing resources of legitimacy (through institutional consensus) and logistical coordination. Yet mayors and municipal governments opposed to large-scale public works may succeed in overcoming their ordinary political differences (as in Val di Susa) but then enter into conflict with provincial and regional institutions that support the projects (both in Val di Susa and the Straits), or clash with other communes in favour of the project (e.g. centre-right-governed communes in the Straits).

Environmental associations are again confirmed to be important protest actors, above all in the initial and incubating phases. They bring technical-scientific knowledge and legitimisation in the eyes of public opinion, thanks to their reputation as national associations, making them difficult to accuse of Nimbyism. They demonstrate a capacity for duration and have a strong knowledge of the informational and procedural strategies to adopt, influencing the public decision-making process through various types of legal action. However, we *see* tensions emerge with other actors involved in the campaign, who accuse environmentalists of being single-issue or privileging alliances with institutional actors (or at least better-structured organisations), as well as adopting transversal alliances from right to left, especially in the area of the Straits.

Citizens' committees are also crucial actors for mobilisation in both protests, though more numerous and decisive in the No Tav campaign. Adopting a flexible and participative organisational structure, they are capable of putting different actors in contact with each other on different themes, reactivating earlier networks of citizens involved in territorial struggles. They mobilise through direct actions (though sometimes discontinued) and opened in the territory through processes of learning. As a spontaneous phenomenon that is weakly structured, they face difficulties in maintaining constant collective involvement over time (Allasino 2004; della Porta 2004a).

Squatted social centres and their militants are central actors in both campaigns, bringing generational resources and political-organisational experiences in practices of direct action and countercultural activities. While often labelled as violent by the press and the authorities, making them "uncomfortable" allies for other activists, the social centres are integrated in protest networks through their participation in mobilisation and a growth in bonds of mutual trust (No Tav), as well as the promotion of initiatives and the formation of coordination networks (No Bridge). Tensions still emerge, particularly in the area of the Straits and with environmental associations; yet these tensions are not so much over repertoires of action as over differing conceptions of participative democracy.

In both our campaigns, the main confederal unions (with the exception of the radical wing of CGIL) are favourable to the two public works, citing their positive impact on employment levels. Yet this does not prevent the growing adherence to the protest of individual workers, who then put pressure upon their own organisations (in a process defined as social appropriation by McAdam et al. 2003), as well as the "critical" unions (Cub, Cobas), which are among the main protagonists, defining the environmental struggle in terms of opposing privatisation (also of space), maintaining employment and addressing issues of public health.

In our cases, the tensions between the different visions held by the different actors were often "solved" in action. It was during the mobilisation that mutual trust developed. The specific resources of the various mentioned actors converged in structures of coordination, which, however, differed in the two campaigns. In Val di Susa, the coordination of mayors, committees, associations and squatted social centres is more or less formalised and stable with an assembly structure. The normative organisational model is of a deliberative type with a consensual decision-making style based on reasoning, shared choices and the search for unanimity, with diversity of opinion being considered a source of richness for the whole movement. Popular participation from below is very high and, while the assembly structure slows decision-making, it also represents an asset by allowing the construction of a common identity. In the area of the Straits, the networks and various coordinations succeed each other chronologically and vary spatially (Sicilian versus Calabrian coast), and tend to be more informal structures, often created ad hoc for specific initiatives and consisting of a small core of activists, who assure the continuity of collective action despite the continual change in official names. If the organisational process is more territorially decentralised, the decision-making process for the larger initiatives is not based on the consensual method but rather on negotiation within the nucleus of core activists and their organisations of reference. There is a clear difference in role between activists, who promote and organise events (demonstrations, campsites, etc.), and citizens, who limit themselves to participation. The relations between the various elements of the protest oscillate between cooperation and competition (della Porta and Diani 1997: 142–45), in a continual tension between the search for unity in action and the recognition of geographical divisions (Sicilian versus Calabrian coast) and political differences (moderate versus radical wing).

The difference between these campaigns can be explained by the varying political and associational traditions in the two geographical areas. The popular involvement of citizens is much higher in Val di Susa, where there is a well-established leftist subculture with a strong tradition of association and participation, creating a high intensity of social capital. In the area of the Straits there is a tendency among citizens to delegate to activists the organisation of protest, and this reflects the weak protest traditions and associational networks in the area, with consequently lower social capital.

We have stressed that the network structure facilitates the convergence of resources from very different groups, and at the same time networking develops in action. The different phases of the protest campaign and their respective duration also affect the form of the organisational networks. Through a process of cross-fertilisation and networking in action, stable and cohesive coordinations are formed in Val di Susa, above all during the phase of direct actions, such as the site occupations (*see* Chapter 4) in response to the implementation of public decision-making (opening of building site, digging works) when the construction of the project is perceived as imminent. In these conditions of opening policy windows, common agreements (or at least a common orientation) are built during the direct action. In the Messina Straits, coordinations and networks are formed, dissolved and re-formed, while protest actions remain more conventional. It can therefore be hypothesised that, if building works begin in the area of the Straits, there will be an acceleration of protest, which would in turn adopt increasingly disruptive forms (direct actions and site occupations), with the formation of a more coherent and stable protest network similar to that found in Val di Susa. In fact, the construction of networks proceeds with the different phases of mobilisation, thus recreating resources for action.

If the network structure testifies to the capacity of adaptation to environmental challenges, we have also stressed that different organisational structures and principles are still present in the mobilisation campaigns. These can facilitate cross-fertilisation, with the development of appeals for participation and deliberation, but may also constitute per se sources of internal tensions.

Notes

1. In early organisational sociology, the closed system approach presented organisations as causal agents: "Internal factors are the prime causal agents in accounting for the structure and behaviour of organizations" (Scott 1983: 156). In the 1960s, an open system approach stressed the technical interdependence of organisations and their environment. More recently, with the neo-institutional approach in organisational theory, there has been a shift of focus from the technical to the sociocultural environment (ibid.: 161). According to proponents of this approach: "The new institutionalism in organizational theory and sociology comprises a rejection of the rational-actor models, an interest in institutions as independent variables, a turn towards cognitive and cultural explanations, and an interest in properties of sovra-individual units of analysis that cannot be reduced to aggregations or direct consequences of individuals' attributes or motives" (DiMaggio and Powell 1991: 8–9).

2. Neo-institutionalism marked a shift from Parson's conception of internalisation (derived from Freudian utilitarianism) to placing an emphasis on cognitive processes, derived from ethno-methodology and phenomenology, with their attention to everyday action and practical knowledge (DiMaggio and Powell 1991: 15ff.). Relevant for this analysis is Bourdieu's notion of habitus as "a system of 'regulated improvisation' or generative rules that represents the (cognitive, affective and evaluative) internalisation by actors of past experiences on the basis of shared typifications of social categories, experienced phenomenally as 'people like us'" (ibid.: 26).

3. As an interviewee underlines: "The Mayor of Messina came to the procession on 22 January, met the mayors of Val di Susa, but could not pledge the support of the whole municipal government."

Chapter 3

Protest and Identity: the Symbolic Construction of Conflict

> It is in essence a problem regarding the overall sustainability or unsustainability of a project, the environmental, economic, social and health implications; and to this list I would add moral implications, as the moral question plays a not indifferent role in this issue. We are faced with situations shaped by clear conflicts of interest, and of no small sum in economic terms; we are talking about more or less explicit deals and collusion between various actors. (IVS 3)

1. Protest and Identity: an Introduction

This interview with a No Tav activist defines the stake of the protest as made of a series of complex problems, with both environmental and social implications, involving public health as well as ethical issues. Research on other conflicts (whether local or not) has underlined the importance of symbolically defining a problem and attributing it a political cause. The mobilisation of citizens into a collective action does not solely depend on the "objective" danger facing their interests, nor does it entirely depend on the availability of structural resources for protest (particularly organisation), but it is closely linked to a subjective component: the awareness of a problem. In the cognitive process of interpreting reality, the actors in a conflict construct and exploit frames of references that "allow individuals to find, conceive, identify and label the events which occur in their lives and more generally in the world at large", thus giving sense to their actions (Snow et al. 1986: 464). In this process, activists have recourse to "evocative cultural symbols, that resonate with those of their potential adherents and are able to motivate them towards collective action" (Vallocchi 2005: 53). Frames of reference are elements of a "cognitive process through which people activate their knowledge in such a way as to interpret an event or a circumstance and locate it within a broader scheme of significance" (Oliver and Johnston 2005: 193). This allows them to attribute meaning to distant events by defining problems as being socially determined, while seeking solutions, hypothesising new social assets, developing new forms of regulation between groups, finding new means to articulate consensus and new ways to exercise power (della Porta and Diani 2006: chap. 3).

From a strategic perspective, protest promoters construct a discourse oriented towards convincing citizens of their legitimate reasons for protest. To achieve this, they use strategies of articulation, which connect various events into a coherent frame, strategies of amplification, which link the specific discourse of protest to more general themes, and strategies of alignment, which link themes of the protest with a series of shared cultural values (Snow et al. 1986). An analysis of the construction of meaning during the course of protest should go beyond the instrumental dimension, and look at the process through which people construct their reality, applying "primary" frames of reference that link daily life and historical events (Johnston 2005). Individual knowledge and collective experience, ideologies, symbols, values are in fact activated in the course of a collective action. This process filters and transforms daily life. History is in fact reconstructed on the basis of everyday experiences; although partly tied to the perception of reality, it is also "manipulated" to give meaning and value to everyday life, which then becomes part of the protest. During protest campaigns a "grammar" emerges, a sort of narrative scheme through which histories, tales and memories are organised so as to understand external reality and act upon it.

In this chapter we shall focus on the effect that the enlargement of the protest networks has on the definition of the identity of protesters, their motivation to protest and their definition of what is at stake in the protest. As a No Tav activist observes, "the wealth of the movement is precisely in this, the capacity, not only ours but of people more generally, of finding a new way to stay together, despite being different" (IVS 1). As we shall see, the growth of the mobilisation is reflected in the tensions (typical of protests against large-scale infrastructural projects) between local identity and global reach, defence of the environment and common goods, demands for administrative decentralisation and participation from below. In the following pages we shall look at the effects of mobilisation on the emergence and evolution of frames relating to the definition of the identity of the actor (section 2), the diagnosis and prognosis of the problem (section 3), and finally the motivation for action (section 4).

2. Framing the Identity: Between Localism and Community

This community of human beings is not a natural product, it is a construction ... half of the *Valsusini* work out of the valley while half of those who work in the valley are not a *Valsusino*: you are a *Valsusino* because you accept certain values, you share a path, nothing ethnic here. The history of the valley is a passing valley, a history that belongs to everybody ... there is the idea of a common destiny. (IVS 2)

As in the words of this trade unionist, a fundamental element for mobilization is the definition of the identity of those who protest, who share values and interests: the "us" opposed to the "them" (Gamson 1988). The definition of identity occurs prior to the definition of the interest, in so far as preferences are constructed by a symbolic process. Only if I define my own identity am I able to name my long-term interest (Pizzorno 1993). In local conflicts, a trend often emerges between the increasing solidarity at the level of the local community (the history of a "passing valley") and the appeal for universal values (to a "common destiny") necessary for the mobilisation of external allies.

A central theme in the discourse of local oppositions to large-scale public works regards the territorial scale of the conflict. The local dimension is stigmatised by supporters of large-scale public works as egotistical. In such a manner, referring to the opposition to the Tav, the former centre-right Minister for the Environment, Matteoli, speaks of the "egotism of an instrumentalised protest" (R 4/11/05) and the centre-left President of the Piedmont regional government, Mercedes Bresso, repeats that "the interest of the few cannot prevail over those of the many" (R 27/11/05), "the important thing is that we overcome the 'I don't want it in my backyard' syndrome: it brings us nowhere" (R 20/11/05). With regard to the protests against the bridge, Minister Matteoli similarly declares that "everybody needs the bridge" and that "the protest is brought by sectoral interests, such as environmentalists or strictly local groups"(GaS 23/1/06).

Defined as localist by their opponents, those who contest large-scale public works frequently underline a communitarian defence of a territory that is suffering from external aggression. In the No Tav protests at the start of 2000, the slogans concentrated on the valley: "A train every 3 minutes, goodnight *Valsusini*", "We want to grow with the green of our valley", "Church of Susa, help us. Tell us the truth." The first objective of the mobilisation is to "save the valley" (R 30/1/00). Still in 2005, the leaflet for coordinating the committees of Val di Susa that calls a site occupation for 3 October appeals against "all those who want to destroy Val di Susa" (DVS 1). This dimension of defence of the community is linked to the identification with the territory, beyond class or ideological divisions – "All united, without educational, economic or political barriers, or municipal divisions", writes an activist (Margaira 2005: 37).

Similarly, in the Straits of Messina there is a communitarian narrative emerges in the defence of a territory perceived as being under attack. In fact, the first appeal of the committee "Between Scilla and Charybdis" in June 1998 called for "wisdom to prevail". Beyond the definitive cancellation of the bridge project this committee also asked the UNESCO "to assume under its protection the area of the Messina Straits, inasmuch as it is an intangible good and the heritage of humanity" (DME 1). Such a dimension of the protest remained unaltered all along the long campaign, with the final appeal of the large demonstration in Messina (22 January 2006) being for "everyone in Messina to defend the Straits", a place that is considered by the promoters to be "unique in the history and the culture of the Mediterranean, which must be defended from interventions whose impact would be irreversible" (DME 18).

However, the appeal to community leads to a symbolic redefinition of its identity. In the Tav protests, as a journalist observes, it is "as if an always denied Val di Susa identity is emerging ... the valley is rediscovering its soul" (R 14/7/05). During the protest campaigns, a positive definition of community emerges, with a stress on its historical, political and cultural particularities (della Porta 2004a, b). Significant in the definition of local identity is the reference to the history of the partisan Resistance against the Nazi occupation in Val di Susa: the President of the Mountainous Community talks of a "valley with a history. Here were the Partisans" (R 9/12/05); the Valsusa Film Festival of 2003 concentrates on the partisan memory (R 18/4/03); at the No Tav demonstration of June 2005 a memorial monument in the Val Cenischia is unveiled, paying homage to the partisans (5/6/05). The partisan past is often evoked, as in the testimony of the will to "resist" shown by the inhabitants of Val di Susa. One of the mayors of the valley (in office for twenty-eight years) recalls: "I was a member of the 42nd Garibaldi Brigade. My motto is 'resist now and for ever'. Yesterday against the Nazi occupation, today against the diggers." During the so called "occupation" of the territory by the police forces, the Mayor of Mompantero affirmed that "I am here to ask for solidarity for our little village. The first to be anti-fascist, the first to be occupied" (R 17/11/05). The activists, who take up the picketing with the slogan "*Suma turna sì*" ("We are back, yes") and "*La Val di Susa resiste*", recall 8 December 1943 in the same valley where the partisan Resistance was born (R 9/12/05). The partisans are recalled in the logo within the No Tav banner; in particular "the old man with the closed fist has been invented by the committee of Bussoleno and recalls the grandfather who fought in the Resistance and who shouted 'You will not pass here'" (IVS 4).

Though less felt than in Val di Susa (for historical and geographical reasons), the references to the identity of the community are also relevant in the area of the Straits. Frequent appeals are made to the Italian *Mezzogiorno* (Italian South), while the activists talk of the "opposition by the people of the Straits", recalling the past battles against the carbon-fuelled reactors in Calabria (DME 21).The communitarian dimension of the protest is recognised (among others) by the Secretary of the Party of Refounded Communists (PRC), Fausto Bertinotti, who affirms that "nowadays many problems do not pass through party channels, they quickly pass straight into the communitarian dimension, they grow through parishes, neighbourhoods and areas. We must take into account this phenomenon of community" (R 7/11/05). Concerning the symbolic construction of the community, the formation of identity during the course of the action is underlined by the activists: "The traditions, the identity counted, but they were elements that were acquired, rather than starting points" (IVS 1).

The reference to community, however, presents the risk of isolation if it is conceived in an exclusive sense. Instead, during the course of mobilisation the search for alliances with external actors brings about a process of "bridging" between local and global identities. It is the same people that oppose the Tav who underline a change in the frames during the evolution of the protest, with a progressive widening of the horizon beyond the valley. According to an activist:

> It is true that the initial opposition to the Tav was at times simplistic and even egotistical: "They will throw me out of my house, they will make me leave the valley, how much value will my house lose?" But then, as administrators and citizens, we understood that we needed less simple arguments that would support our initial opposition. So we found some experts, university professors, who confirmed to us what we feared. The damage from the noise of a high-speed train, for example, or those following from years and years (twenty according to the plan) of having lorries in our streets. And dust, traffic and pollution. (Margaira 2005: 118)

In fact, in the course of the protest, instrumental frames leave the way for ethical ones. An activist observes that "this is not a party question, or only an environmental one, it is an ethical and moral question, but we at first did not realise that" (ibid.). The rhetoric and perception of what is at stake escalate together with the belief that the protest is not being listened to. During the campaign, "when we clearly understood that we would never have a voice in decisions taken elsewhere, then the contestation became really tough, our certainties strengthened, and we automatically realised that at risk was not only our territory ... at risk was the death of a countryside and the founding system of collectivity: ethics, reciprocal respect" (ibid.: 123). Differently than in most US voluntary groups studied by Nina Eliasoph (1998), where appeals to the public opinion were mainly apolitical in order to adapt to the dominant mood, in our cases the protest discourse became immediately political. In particular, with the territorial scale shift in the target of the protest, there is a growth in the generality of the discourse on causes and solutions of the perceived problem.

A scale shift is emerging in particular in the most recent stages: the No Tav campaign clearly assumes a global dimension. According to an interviewee, "there is here the first, concrete no global struggle, not only in Italy but also at European level. We do not say it, we do not like labels, but this is a no global struggle, because we oppose an international project that passes over the rights of local communities" (IVS 11). In a similar manner, on the Straits, "an important soul of the No Bridge movement is tied to the larger movement against neoliberal globalisation, with different ways and features of course" (IME 4). References to global struggles are frequent in the protesters' documents, in their strategic thinking and in the symbols chosen.

3. Diagnosis and Prognosis: What Progress?

> In contrast to liberalist enunciations on the centrality of the market, it is public money (subtracted from public services) that is used to realise these large-scale public works (bridges, highways, tunnels, dams, power plants) ... which are then given, through privatisation, to economic groups that are collateral to the political class, whose essential contribution is to store away the profits. So then we have a repeat of the traditional passage, public money – private profit. On this level it is evident that there is a convergence in the interests of powerful financiers, businessmen, politicians and the Mafia, whose intertwining is now no longer a crime or even a scandal. (DME 3)

This text taken from a document elaborated by No Bridge activists, recalls another central feature of the symbolic construction of the conflict: the definition (not only in a negative sense) of what is at stake. The definition of the "us" is strictly linked to the heart of the conflict. Snow and Benford (1988) talk of diagnostic frames, oriented to develop a new image of what is wrong, and prognostic frames, which suggest solutions for the identified problems.

Traditionally, the opponents of LULUs have been said to privilege the value of their environment (value of use) against "growth machines" that stress the sole importance of economic development (value of exchange). In this image, residents have an inherent interest in defending their quality of life (health, cultural heritage), while economic investors (and often local politicians) push for their economic (or political) interests to be pursued. The strength of the growth machines has been seen in their capacity to convince residents that economic development would have a positive spillover on their life as well. As Gould et al. (1996: 5) stated:

> Environmental conflicts are fundamentally struggles over the different capacities of social groups to meet their needs by gaining access to natural resources. One of the dilemmas in managing ecological scarcity in a liberal industrial society is the need to satisfy the demands of private capital and public agencies for economic growth, as well as the demands of citizens for maintaining public health and maintaining the recreational and aesthetic amenities of their natural habitat.

However, the definition of the interest of the citizen results from a symbolic struggle. The very conception of the public interest is the object of a symbolic struggle between Tav and bridge opponents and supporters.

In our two case studies, opponents of large-scale public works are caricatured by proponents of these projects as displaying "archaic prejudices and cultural backwardness or instrumentalisation and political bad faith". This feature is also evident in similar conflicts (*see* Borelli 1999: 39). One of the frames used against those who protest is in fact their assumed opposition to progress. With regard to the anti-Tav struggle, the centre-right politician Confalonieri (Forza Italia) speaks of a "retrograde opposition to a work that is fundamental for the progress of the country" (R 30/11/05), while the National Secretary of the Democrats of the Left, Piero Fassino, believes that "there is a cultural problem: we must struggle against anti-scientific thinking, the irrationality that generates fear" (R 7/2/05) as "often the objections are daughters of a regressive culture" (R 23/11/05). With respect to the anti-bridge protests, Folco Quilici, a famous documentary film-maker of marine fauna favourable to the bridge and from April 2005 member of the governing board of SdM, defines the struggle against the bridge as "obscurantist: we cannot imagine the world can progress without constructions of this type. Rome was a village of brigands before the *Campidoglio* was realised or the bridge on the Tiber" (GaS 23/1/06). Likewise, SdA responds to the No Bridge objections by claiming that their "criticisms are based on slogans without foundations that are either technical, environmental, socio-economic or financial. They are in fact statements that contrast with the facts, with what is stipulated in the project, with the approval from the competent authorities, with the valuation of the government, the Italian Parliament and the European Parliament" (GdS 22/1/06). In *La Repubblica* newspaper, the journalist Sebastiano Messina writes that "the people of Val di Susa have all the right to defend their health ... another discussion must be made for ... the professionals of 'No'. Those who oppose the Bridge on the Straits because it interrupts the flight of the storks" (R 8/12/05).

The central theme for supporters of large-scale public works is in fact development: locally facing a decline in terms of competitiveness, and more broadly (national, European) requiring large strategic projects. Significantly, the director of the committee promoting the Transpadana railway argues against those who "prejudice the interests of the Turinese, Piedmontese, Italian and European communities" (R 22/3/05). At the local level, the large-scale works are presented – in Piedmont, as in Calabria and Sicily – as necessary to break out of geographical isolation. The President of the province of Turin (centre-left) makes an appeal to "create a true and proper Turinese and Piedmontese lobby that involves all social, political and economic forces, and can put pressure on the government in the competition with other Italian territories" (R 8/6/05). The regional councillor Borioli insists that "the infrastructure is indispensable for getting Piedmont out of the cul-de-sac in which it currently finds itself" (R 25/6/05), while a Minister of the new centre-left national government, Pierluigi Bersani (Ds), affirms that "without a Turin–Lyon, the loss would be above all for the West of Italy", given that the Tav "is a European choice that responds to a grand design" (R 3/11/05). In a public appeal, Piedmontese intellectuals and professionals define the Tav as a strategic opportunity for improving the competitiveness of the region (R 9/7/05). Similar positions are adopted by economic interest associations such as the Confederazione Nazionale Artigianato –(CNA: "National Handicraft Confederation"), which affirms that "the infrastructure is necessary and must be realised to support the competitiveness of firms" and that "the Tav is necessary to avoid isolation because economic centres are those where the arteries of communication pass" (R 16/11/05), while Assoespressi (representing transport associations) claims that without the Tav they will lose 100,000 jobs (R 20/11/05). The Piedmontese secretary of the CGIL union, on the occasion of a strike in the valley against the Tav, underlines that "the strike is a weapon that must be used in a struggle with common objectives. The question of Val di Susa, unfortunately, has always fewer of these characteristics because it risks isolating that collectivity from the general will" (R 5/11/05). At the national level, in a bipartisan manner, a leader of the centre-left coalition, Francesco Rutelli (Margherita), affirms that "the Tav is a fundamental work for the country. The project must be improved, but the commitment to modernise the country must be maintained" (R 2/12/05), and the former President of the House of Deputies, Pierferdinando Casini (centre-right), observes that "the protests in Val di Susa effectively cut us out of the large European infrastructure networks" (R 2/12/05).

Those who support the project of the Bridge on the Messina Straits also define it as essential, not only for the economic development of the interested area, but for the whole Italian South. The former centre-right national government strongly supported the bridge, the Minister for Infrastructure, Pietro Lunardi, defining it as "a fundamental project for our South, strategic for communication links with Northern Europe and the Mediterranean" (Me 13/3/04), "an epoch-making work. The largest of the twenty-first century ... the *Mezzogiorno* must return to connect the two shores of our sea. The Bridge on the Straits is part of that design ... thanks to which the South will return to the centre of the Mediterranean" (CdS 22/4/04). Of the same opinion is the leader of the Forza Italia group in the Senate, Renato Schifani, who defines the bridge as a work that will favour "the development of the South" (Me 13/3/04). Even some local politicians underline the potential for economic development. The centre-right Mayor of Reggio Calabria, Giuseppe Scopelliti, affirms that "the Bridge on the Straits is necessary to the development of the South ... the benefits produced by the bridge will comfortably surpass the social costs tied to its realisation ... the externalities produced by a real shock from this infrastructure will provide a lasting drive to improving the economically weak productive structure existing in the South" (Io 13/3/04). A former councillor in the Commune of Messina (with responsibility for the environment), Elvira Amata (centre-right) maintains that "we must reason in terms of the development of the city: the project will bring well-being, tourists and employment" (A 6/10/03). Also the President of the Province of Catania, Raffaele Lombardo (leader of the centre-right "Movement for Autonomy"), declares that we need "to quickly build the bridge, which is the mother of all infrastructures, which will then make indispensable other infrastructural projects, and not the reverse" (CdS 8/12/05); and finally the political scientist Angelo Panebianco insists that the principal reason for supporting the bridge is that it represents "the possibility for victory of a Sicily and a South that exist and that would like to build a future of self-sustaining development" (CdS 5/12/05) that is "normal and European, archiving away the Mafia and the anti-Mafia" (CdS 8/12/05). The symbolic aspect of the bridge is often underlined as a "redemption of the South" (R 2/10/03), with former Minister Lunardi maintaining that "the Bridge on the Straits is a work worthy of the Roman Empire ... a symbol. The sign that a spirit is returning, that of the great builders" (CdS 22/4/04).

In relation to these appraisals of the project, those who protest against the Tav and the bridge clearly risk stigmatisation. A first counter-strategy is to affirm the necessity to privilege well-being (value of use of the territory) above economic development (value of exchange). The defence of public health is claimed, citing the various appeals of doctors from Val di Susa who have highlighted the risks of tumours developing from either the asbestos (mesothelioma) or the uranium (lymphoma) that can be found in the ground that is to be dug – in their appeal, the doctors conclude that "there is the real possibility of severe damage to public health" (DVS 2).

The image of living in the past and opposing progress is contested by opponents of these projects, who develop an alternative model of economic development. First of all, the quality of life is defended against projects that are defined as pharaonic, anti-economic and useless, in addition to damaging for the territory involved. The anti-economic aspect of the work is stated by underlining its incompatibility with regard to the characteristics of local development – from tourism tied to agriculture to fishing. In an appeal to a general strike in Val di Susa we read that "if the ecosystem is destroyed so will be the economic structure of the area. The damage would be incalculable. The pollution caused by the asbestos powder would place in crisis the agricultural small and medium-sized industries of the area" (DVS 5). Besides, the protesters underline – citing data on the current use of the railway network and projections for future demand – the uselessness of building another line (the counter-proposal is therefore a much cheaper restructuring of the existing line). Commenting on electoral results that saw the No Tav list gain around 10 per cent in the valley (where all candidates of all parties anyway expressed their opposition to the Tav), the meteorologist Mercalli underlines that "we are not talking about nine thousand small landowners that fear expropriation, but nine thousand citizens that maintain the project to be useless and damaging" (R 17/6/04). Even eleven Piedmontese regional councillors from left-wing parties (PRC, PdCI and the Greens) have demanded that the Tav be re-negotiated, given the excessive economic cost and the devastating environmental impact (R 23/5/05).The enviromantalist association Legambiente recalls that a Loetschenberg tunnel between Berne and Sempione is being opened, and in 2015 one in Gottardo will be opened as well; the two tunnels will absorb in large part the traffic of goods (R 4/6/05), while the WWF defines the Tav as "a hazard from the economic and transportational point of view" (R 4/6/05).

Similarly, the No Bridge activists speak of a:

> useless work, anti-economic and devastating, from a wrong era and in the wrong place. It could have been a good idea 40, 30 or 20 years ago, because it was a work that for better or worse had a certain "image", but currently there is a situation that pushes not only Europe, but the whole world, to rely on transport via sea, reducing the consumption of petrol, of car traffic, privileging forms of transport that are much less damaging than cars, and they want to realise a road right in the middle of the only sea in Europe where there isn't one! It seems to be pure folly. It is a work that has been imagined in a territory where, in the meantime, there has been a certain development; so they pretend that the city should have to adapt to the bridge rather than the bridge to the city. (IME 1)

In addition, opponents denounce the damage the bridge would bring to local economic activity, without bringing any lasting increases in employment as promised by those in favour of the project.

The promise of jobs is disputed by activists who fore*see* a negative employment balance. An activist of the "CariddiScilla" coordination declares that "the people of Messina, of the Straits, have discovered that the bridge barely interests them and it goes against their local interests, because it can only lose jobs, and is useless from the point of view of increasing employment" (IME 2). In a flyer of the critical union Cobas, we read that, "in the jungle of the neoliberal market, investment does not produce work, but only profit. Unless by work we mean the exploitation of the precarious workers with the hours of a slave, without rights or protection" (DVS 7).

In denouncing the economic damage of large-scale public works to local development, the alternative use of the territory is underlined (more socially just and ecologically sustainable), together with a different use of the funds allocated to the large-scale public works. In the pro-Tav and pro-bridge discourse, the two projects are defined as "no-cost", because financed externally (e.g. European Union or private companies). Investments in the Tav or in the bridge are never considered alongside possible alternatives, while it is continually repeated that there is a risk of losing EU funding destined for precisely those projects. The protesters instead denounce the waste of resources that could be better utilised. According to a politician of the valley, "Why not improve the old railway, today underused, for goods and commuters? The entrepreneurs who fight for Tav are private actors, but public money will be spent" (R 12/8/05). The high investment in visible works therefore becomes linked to the loss of essential services: "They cut services to invest in large-scale public works", "They cut personnel in the stations and on trains" (R 3/12/03). In the flyer calling for a demonstration on 17 December we can read that "public money is necessary first of all to improve local transport, social and health services, for research and for all those important things that instead they are cutting" (DVS 6). In the general strike at the end of November 2005, the No Tav protestors bring a banner that reads "15 billion for the Tav! And for work in Val di Susa?" (R 26/11/05).

The same discussion also applies to those who oppose the bridge. An activist of WWF denounces the:

> insane costs to the state, even if they say these are private funds, up till now there haven't been any. They are funds left by IRI that should have gone to the Treasury but instead are going to the SdM group, so it is public money. All of this despite other more impelling needs, the basic needs necessary to live in a dignified and civil way, for which they claim not to have a euro. It makes me laugh when they say that 200 trains a day will pass over the bridge, and I ask myself: to go where, given how the train system works in Sicily? (IME 1)

No bridge activists ask (in various appeals for demonstration) that the sum allocated for the construction of the bridge (6 billion euros) is instead invested in "adapting and strengthening the existing infrastructure in Calabria and Sicily" (DME 18), and in particular in "improving sustainable maritime mobility and reclaiming the coasts" (DME 13).

To those who define them as backward and isolationist, the protesters respond with a definition of themselves as being aware of the future. The flyer calling for the march from Susa to Venaus on 4 June 2005 invites "all to Susa to defend the future of our territory" (DVS 3). In parallel, the No Bridge activists observe that "they say that we are 'backward' and 'against the future', as if a bridge of cement and steel were the future, given that they were being built 80 years ago, when people were still thinking about the society of automobiles" (IME 4). The reference to the future is in effect a tool of legitimacy, particularly when referring to future generations and a global dimension.

The symbolic challenge therefore concerns the very definition of progress. If those who propose large-scale public works define their investments as leading to progress, those who oppose them propose instead a different definition of progress: a human progress, which is counterposed to an inhuman economic progress. In the Val di Susa diocesan journal, it can be read that "the inhabitants of Val di Susa are not idiots. None of them wants to stop progress. They simply pose the following question to the whole country. What is the price that we must pay for this progress, for this development?" (R 6/11/05). Among the Tav supporters, the promise of jobs from the project becomes contrasted with an "evil" occupation. While the secretary of the Union of Builders talks of the "folly of thinking that the Tav, a work of 15 years, will not bring development", the petition of the Val di Susa unions for an anti-Tav strike remembers past experiences with large-scale public works as providing only "precarious work, under oppressive conditions", and calling for alternative uses of the funds invested in the Tav (e.g. international universities) (R 8/11/05). Similarly, in the Cobas flyer calling for a strike on 16 November, we read that the union criticises neoliberal market economy as oriented to produce profits through the hyper-exploration of precarious workers, deprived of basic labour rights (DVS 7). With an appeal to a different notion of progress, the anarchists of FAI call for "a more livable environment for a civilisation founded on people and not on profit, on the quality of life and not its speed" (DVS 8). The petition of workers in the Val di Susa, entitled "Let us decide our own future", denounces a "propaganda that tries to spread the idea that the Tav can increase employment and will bring economic benefits to the inhabitants", maintaining the importance of "having an idea of sustainable development that is compatible with environmental needs and the health of citizens". The secretary of the critical union Cub refutes "the idea that any job, in any condition, is an objective for which everything else must be sacrificed" (IVS 2).

The No Tav and No Bridge protesters also propose a critique of consumption, which echoes the "no growth" discourse, synthesised in the slogan to "consume less, consume better". Luca Mercalli, activist and meteorologist, affirms that "we cannot think of a world where economic growth continues. High-speed trains consume energy, in a world where energy is exhausting itself, destroying agricultural fields and historic sites" (R 4/6/05). Legambiente also stigmatises the blind faith in progress and ignorance of its consequences, its first slogan being that "we love the train too much to accept the Tav" (R 12/8/05). A representative of the Greens also observes that "it is not only a confrontation between alternative models of transport, but between alternative models of development: here we have to begin to ask what goods to produce, why to transport them and where to" (IVS 3). In the interviews with activists, the search for an alternative model of development emerges, which goes beyond the definition of "sustainable development" and calls for a "low-speed life". As an interviewee from Val di Susa observes, "we are in opposition to the same old model, the violent way to impose their interests, we want to live a low-speed life, decently: we do not think that time is money, that is a principle of bosses, time serves to live well while work must also be a tool to live well" (ISV 10).

At stake here is the very definition of development. According to the metalworkers' union Fiom, "We are the victims of a single model of development. But it no longer convinces us. No one has explained what goods the Turin–Lyon line will move, for what companies and for what reasons. They start from a dogmatic assumption, namely that this work is strategic and fundamental, but the reasons are not explained" (R 8/11/05). In an appeal by the Piedmontese trade unionists for a demonstration on 17 December, the No Tav issue is cited not only with respect to the democratic deficit and the undervaluation of the environmental damage, but also because it "requires an immediate reflection by the entire union movement on this model of development, on the costs and benefits connected to it, that the interests of the populations and the workers should not be subordinated to those of goods and the global market". A priest in the site occupation affirms that "the Italian constitution guarantees the health of the citizen, this project does not. For this reason I define it as inhumane" (R 3/11/05).

In the struggle against the Bridge on the Straits, the definition of development is likewise placed under scrutiny. In a document we read that "the notion of 'development' that is continuously being imposed implies waste, incinerators, thermoelectric plants, large-scale public works, with claims that these projects will be able to provide work for the poor unemployed in the South" (DME 6). But, as a No bridge activist points out, the mobilisation against the bridge "was necessary to relaunch our perspective on how this territory should be managed. In fact, the opposition to the bridge is linked to a revaluation of the countryside, environment, and even the resources in the area of the Straits" (IME 4).

Together with the notion of progress, there is the concept of a general or national interest that is being contested. The sociologist Luciano Gallino notes that:

> we need to ask ourselves if it is not precisely the inhabitants of Val di Susa who, with their opposition to the Tav project, are carrying out the national interest. That they pursue particularistic interests is not in doubt. But in doing so they have led to the emergence in Italy of a mass of studies, documents and questions founded on the validity and priority of the project, to make us think that a minimal level of precaution should lead us to take them into serious consideration. (R 7/11/05)

On the other side of the protest, an activist declares, "We are against those who accuse us of Nimbyism, for which our particularistic interest would be opposed to a general interest, to the common good. We need to define what is meant by common good, because here we are talking about old-fashioned speculative operations, in this case a classic showpiece construction project" (IME 4).

In contrast large-scale public works are presented as benefiting only the few – "moneymakers", "speculators" or even the "corrupt" and "Mafiosi". The supporters of the Tav are defined as "businessmen" (DVS 10), and the "pro-Tav lobby" as "gigantic speculators" (DVS 7). It is "a great idea for bricklayers or, as we call them, the 'lobby of the reinforcing rod', which has decided that this work will certainly bring a lot of money into their business and so they developed this project and sold it to the politicians ... so we end up with a transversal right–left lobby in favour of it" (IVS 5). The bridge is presented as "a business for a few people ... *the lobby of cement*, the club of large-scale public works transversally tied to political parties and accustomed to portioning, to cross-presences that nullify controls and competition, to despoiling resources (Mangano and Mazzeo 2006: 14). The role of the Mafias emerges "in two ways: the role of local crime in controlling the work through subcontracts, and the attempt to finance directly the work, already attempted by the international Mafia" (ibid.).

4. Motivational Frames: the Rights of the Community, Mobilisation of the People

> It does not matter if we win at the end, it is important to think that we can do things: the feeling we had to fight against was: "They will do it all the same." It is not important that David wins, but that he has bridled Goliath for 5 minutes: if you bridled him for 5 minutes, you can bridle him for 5 hours and you cannot be beaten. (IVS 9)

The struggle between David and Goliath recalled in this interview is often quoted in the analysis of local conflicts. An important function of the framing process is indeed producing motivations to action – i.e. giving people a reason to join the protest by convincing them that collective action is not only possible but also potentially successful (Snow and Benford 1988). In this process, the stakes of the conflict expand to the meta-frames of democracy, as well as the right to protest (della Porta 1999). As in other territorial conflicts, in our two cases the discourse extends itself to procedural issues: "those opposing are able to transform the nature of the problem: what is questioned is no longer only the danger of the project, but also the correct procedure that led to the decision about the localisation of the project" (Bobbio 1999: 189). Typically in local conflicts the rights of the local population to decide on large-scale public works is a principal issue at stake. Our cases confirm that, when there is an open discussion on LULUs, the project "is normally already tied to a specific site. They can discuss how, but not 'where'" (ibid.: 193) – or in our cases they may discuss "how" but not "if" – and a discursive strategy used by the promoters of large-scale public works is to present them as an "accomplished fact". Those who oppose these works must therefore articulate in a credible manner a discourse that points towards action, by accentuating a sense of injustice, and by spreading the belief that an alternative is possible.

In the case of Val di Susa, it is above all the Piedmontese and national politicians of the centre-left (particular Democrats of the Left, Ds) who seek to limit the role of the mayors of Val di Susa, who are all against the Tav. The President of the Piedmontese Region, Mercedes Bresso (Ds), claims that:

> the decision on whether the work will be undertaken is a decision for Europe, the two states involved, and the two regions involved. The choice on how to do it, with what guarantees for the population involved, with which characteristics for the building sites, is a choice that must involve the inhabitants and the local politicians of Val di Susa. (R 15/11/05)

As mentioned (*see* above) in a similar manner, the SdA group replies to the No Bridge opponents by suggesting that the project has been approved by the Italian government and the European Parliament, the unique competent authorities legitimatised to take decisions; in addition, pro-bridge consider their objections not founded, from financial, technical and environmental viewpoints. (GdS 22/1/06).

In reaction to this, one of the first frames used in Val di Susa by those protesting underlines the rights of the local politicians to represent their territory. In the demonstration of 30 May 2002, the President of the Mountainous Communities (Ferrentino, also Ds) insists that "they cannot ignore the views of locally elected officials" (R 1/6/03). In autumn 2003, the No Tav committee announces a recourse against "a project imposed by Rome without the involvement of local officials" (R 12/11/03). And in a flyer we read that "the communities of the valley affected by the project have had no say. Once again the mountain people are there to be squeezed into servitude" (R 30/11/03). Reunited for the entire day in Piazza Castello (Turin), thirty-seven local councillors ask for the involvement of local bodies, protesting at not having been even minimally involved (R 20/3/05).

Although local politicians in the Messina Straits are divided in their attitude with respect to the bridge, the inclusion of local communities in the decision-making process is often called for. According to a WWF activist, the bridge "violates all democratic norms. The Objective Law is anything but democratic: they passed it to realise more quickly their public works, but they excluded local communities from the decision-making process; which is a folly, because you victimise people, set up building sites there for decades, and don't even ask them if they agree to it" (IME 1). The claim becomes the right to self-determination – not to be dealt with as a colony: "The problem is to change the criteria by which choices become imposed in the territory, as if they were colonies, whereas we are firmly convinced that territories must be subject to the judgement of the people who inhabit them, and that they should decide their own programme and their own future" (IME 4).

With a shift from a specific decision to the meta-issue of how decisions should be made, the lack of democratic procedure in the allocation of large-scale public works is denounced by both No Tav and No Bridge activists; yet the development of a meta-discourse on democracy goes beyond the involvement of local politicians and populations. It is here the very conception of democracy that is placed under scrutiny. The demand for democracy is a demand for another type of democracy – more participative and coming "from below". In the No Tav protest, the rights of the community to decide their own fate are claimed in the name of the people – it is no coincidence that the organisers choose names such as "Committee for the popular struggle against high-speed trains" or *Spinta dal Bass* ("Push from below"). During the march of 15,000 against the "militarisation" of Val di Susa, a participant declared on the megaphone: "It is immoral to keep all these men here to guard a peaceful valley. This is not an emergency, this is participatory democracy" (R 6/11/05). A document of the Southern Network for a New Municipalism reads: "What is attacked as a particularistic interest – whether it be of the community of Val di Susa or the area of the Straits – is instead the expression of the sovereignty of the people who live within that territory, reclaiming their legitimacy to decide their future and that of their children" (DME 16). In this discourse, participatory democracy does not exclude representative democracy, but modifies the conception of "representation", disconnecting it from that of "delegation". As an anti-Tav university professor puts it:

> Participatory democracy is not always easy. It is easier for citizens to give delegation, because they no longer have to think, for politicians to have delegation, because they do not have to repeat the same thing three times: they do the common good, but only a few make decisions. Participatory democracy means to have ideas, but before realising them talking with citizens in an assembly. (IVS 9)

The theme of democracy re-emerges in the defence of protest as a legitimate form of participation, in opposition to the stigmatisation of the protesters as violent. The frame of violence is utilised in particular by the Pro-Tav in autumn 2005, with the growth in forms of direct action. According to the former Minister of the Interior, Giuseppe Pisanu, subversive groups are infiltrating the protest (R 13/11/05). The potential infiltration by radical black blockers justifies, according to the minister, the tough intervention of the police to break the picket because "the risk of infiltration was known to everyone and we had to do things in a hurry" (R 8/12/05). Successively, while apologising to the inhabitants of Val di Susa that were victims of the police assault, he affirms that "those who use violence must either be suffered or confronted", warning of "the subversive nature of the social centres. Of the antagonists. Of the anarcho-insurrectionalists and the anarchist squatters." Even the theme of danger to public security echoes on both Right and Left. On the Right, the former Prime Minister, Silvio Berlusconi, alleges that "antagonistic extreme left groups and anarcho-insurrectionalists are trying to extend the disorder from Val di Susa to Turin, Milan, Rome and various other cities" (R 8/12/05). On the Left, the national secretary of the Ds, Piero Fassino, condemns the "violent methods of the anti-Tav protesters", who are attacking "a well-considered project that will guarantee development, growth, work and well-being" (R 7/11/05).

A symbolic conflict on the right to participate in a democracy emerges around the conception of legality. For the pro-Tav politicians in Piedmont, the protest becomes illegitimate if it opposes the decisions of the (representatives of the) majority. The President of the Piedmont Region, Mercedes Bresso (Ds), affirms that "democracy works like this. You discuss issues and then, without abandoning your initial views, you must accept the decision of the majority. If someone does not want to do that, and instead decides to lay bombs, they exclude themselves from civil society" (R 11/5/05). A similar position is taken by the Mayor of Turin, Sergio Chiamparino, who states that "we have arrived at a point where ... we must allow the rule of the majority to prevail" (R 1/11/05).

The Pro-Tav tend in fact to single out the good from the bad protesters. The former Minister of the Interior, Giuseppe Pisanu, distinguishes between "peaceful protesters and those seeking to do everything to provoke violence", then affirming that "in Val di Susa there is a worrying mix of legitimate popular protest, political speculation and subversive intrusions, which risks exploding from one day to another" (he then cites Al-Qaeda cells, anarchists and autonomist groups) (R 3/12/05). In a similar manner, the centre-left Mayor of Torino, Sergio Chiamparino, maintains that a part of the picketers "are thugs, and I want the protesters' coalition to isolate them before the demonstrations", defining himself as being "in favour of pluralism, as long as you do not consider modernising the city" (R 9/12/05).

Although less than in Val di Susa, the frame of violence and illegality has been used also by the supporters of the bridge. Some No Bridge activists remember that the daily *La Gazzetta del Sud*, one of the main supporters and sponsors of the bridge, has accused the "eco-pacifists" opposed to the bridge of having carried out a series of explosions, realised without damage to people or buildings, in February 2004. An activist recalls that:

> a morning two years ago on the coast of Messina, seven bottles that were loaded with explosives suddenly ignited, making it seem as if there had been a plan. And then something very serious happened: the *Gazzetta del Sud* filled its pages with accusations that these were carried out by "eco-pacifists" opposed to the bridge. This was launching a very precise message. Then the issue was over because they discovered it was four idiots who had exploded the devices to steal some government maritime property. But I am not convinced by this, because I think that behind this there was an attempt to end the protests against the bridge. (IME 3)

And another No Bridge interviewee remembers that "they threw mud at us, saying that it was the movement against the bridge, which had nothing to do with it; and then they found those responsible, who had nothing to do with us, but in the process they sought to portray us as terrorists" (IME 1). The spectre of violence was also raised by the former City Council of Messina (centre-right), which, according to a protester, "two years ago, using the local police, recommended all the shop-owners to close during the procession because they feared acts of violence, the "assault of the barbarians", the black bloc! We obviously derided this, and made a highly communicative procession and most of the shop-owners who did not close then benefited enormously" (IME 4).

The law-and-order frame is defined by those who oppose large infrastructures as instrumental to discrediting an opposition that has persistently chosen peaceful means. The thesis of "bad protesters" is refuted by No Tav, who quote the mass participation in the protests (*see* Chap. 4). An anti-Tav protester complains of having voted for Bresso, who spoke of bombs ("the worst of the Right never amounted to so much"), after:

> fifteen years of full transparency, fifteen years of opposition made by scrutinising the plans of the project. Fifteen years of informational evenings, debates, conferences, fifteen years where not a single stone has been thrown by anyone in the movement. The experience of the No Tav in Val di Susa has been defined as a great building site for participatory democracy, we have grown, aged, inevitably personal relations have intertwined in the movement. Stories of a struggle, because it is a struggle dealing with public life, for free and after having worked all day, it is tiring to participate, to make politics from below. Val di Susa did not deserve this vulgarity ... Lady, without false modesty, we can teach people what active citizenship means. Twenty thousand people in a procession, thirty-five communal councils in Turin, to do something never seen before, decide in Piazza Castello. (Chiara Sasso, R 22/5/05)

Another interviewee remembers: "in response to criminalisation Beppe Grillo [a famous comic actor involved in environmental campaigns] remembered when, during a demonstration, he pointed to an elderly woman shouting: 'You, anarcho-insurrectionalist, what are you doing here?' The limits of the ridiculous have been overcome" (IVS 3). In a similar manner, the support of local politicians is considered as having a strong legitimising value, reducing the credibility of those who describe the protesters as violent.

In discussion here is the possibility to intervene in politics as citizens. In *La Repubblica*, the force of interest groups in favour of the Tav is seen as decisive:

> High-speed, the prerogative or the damnation of our times, will not stop in front of a barricade of stones and trees placed by the people of

Val di Susa: for the simple reason that whether they like it or not, the weight of interests – and here we are discussing legitimate interests, that is the need to connect Italy more rapidly to France and to Europe, to modernize our rail infrastructure, to reach the next station of technological progress – will prevail against all doubts and reserves, against any local resistance. (R 2/11/05)

To this the committees respond that, "when the ants agree, they can move elephants" (R 16/11/05). Defending their right to protest in Turin (whose Mayor had sought to revoke the march on 17 December, stating that there were not "the conditions for a peaceful protest"), a mayor of the valley repeats that "it was precisely the large demonstrations that allowed the possibility of mediation" (R 9/12/05). At the end of the mobilisation, the efficacy of the protest is in fact recognised, among others, in *La Repubblica*:

> It was necessary that an entire valley went into the streets, armed with banners and placards, to finally open a table of negotiation, which in reality should have been open from the start ... now around the table will ideally be seated all the interested Italian citizens, in order to ascertain whether the railway line Turin–Lyon corresponds to the national interest, if it is proportional to the predicted increase in traffic, if it is practical, how many economic resources it requires, and what advantages it offers. (R 12/12/05)

The right to protest is here defended not only as a legitimate right, but also as ethically commendable – "Our force is the anger of the meek" (R 3/12/03). The petition of the Turin Committee expressing support for Val di Susa (DVS 6) invites us to find "the famous grain of sand capable of stalling the powerful motor", praising the "great lesson of participatory democracy" in Val di Susa. As an activist writes, "We do not have hope, we do have certainties; we are only grains of sand but we are many, we have no secondary aims, we are not against progress and in this campaign we have made very few mistakes" (Margaira 2005: 132).

It is precisely on the meta-frame of the right to protest that the statements of solidarity for *Valusini* multiply beyond the valley. Numerous national associations promote a petition to "block the unacceptable violence against the protesters", defending "their democratic right to protest in a peaceful manner" (DVS 16) against a "project that is wrong and to which the overwhelming majority of the local population is opposed". In the words of a provincial councillor of the Greens, "the truncheon blows we took have finally brought into evident light the problem. The problem emerged in the valley, but it does not belong to the valley" (IVS 3). And, on the issue of a different democracy, these protests also brought about the alliance between Val di Susa and the area of the Messina Straits.

5. Concluding Remarks

In this chapter our attention focused on framing processes, which we conceived as being not only important strategic instruments for mobilisation, but also a mechanisms of fundamental importance in the construction of the identity of those who protest. We have in fact suggested that the opposing portrayals of LULU conflicts either as egotistical Nimby protests or as expressive mobilisations of a social conflict on the relative value of use or exchange of territory both consider the values/interests/preferences of actors as being exogenous, concentrating instead on the capacity of these interest representatives to mobilise organisational resources and allies.

In our analysis, we have instead focused on the emergence of these values/interests/preferences through a symbolic conflict that itself defines the collective identities, the stakes of the conflict and the motivations for action. Using categorisations on symbolic construction developed in the literature on social movements, we have in fact analysed the tensions around three important levels of defining the actor and the action. First of all, in the definition of the identity of the actor we can observe on the one hand an elaboration of the positive identity of the community (strongest above all in Val di Susa, around the idea of a valley that resists a "useless and damaging" public work, as it had in the past resisted fascism), and on the other hand a search for universal values, finally arriving at a global definition of the conflict. Against their opponents who accuse them of manifesting the Nimby syndrome, the protesters tend to respond through a symbolic construction that values the community, but without making it an objective of exclusive identification. In this process, and differently than in cases of de-politicization described elsewhere (Eliasoph 1998), a political definition of the conflict emerges.

In search of a definition for the public good, the framing of the dispute tends to supersede the dichotomy between defence of nature and defence of economic development, by constructing an alternative model of progress. While the themes of the health of citizens and the value of the natural environment are both present (as in many other local conflicts), significant attention is focused on defining the struggle as being one oriented to the future rather than to the past. To those who accuse them of wanting to block "large-scale public works" that are "strategic" for local and global economic development, those who protest in Val di Susa and the Messina Straits respond by presenting these works as damaging not only people's health and nature, but economic progress. By opposing a single model of economic development focused on large-scale investments, they underline the value of local economies, and even propose models of "de-development" in order to defend not only the environment, but also levels of employment and quality of life. With regard to projects that are frequently defined as being "cost-free", because they are presented as externally financed, those who oppose these two "large-scale public works" underline the waste of public money, and crucially suggest alternative uses for these resources. It is thus the conception of general interest that is at the centre of these symbolic conflicts, where activists reject the accusations of egotism (typical of the Nimby syndrome). In the discourse of the protesters, the strategic interests defended by the promoters of these "large-scale public works" are presented as being the interests of speculators (corrupted in Val di Susa, Mafiosi in the Messina Straits), while the protesters propose themselves as the true interpreters of the general interest.

Last but not least, the motivational frames underline the possibility of changing decisions, which are often presented as being "already taken", through the collective mobilisation of citizens. Together with the assertion of a political decentralisation that takes into account the rights of local communities to take decisions that will affect their own destiny, there is the increasingly explicit affirmation of a different conception of democracy, based on participation rather than delegation, and privileging protest over voting. This "good" politics is presented as coming from below, made by citizens rather than professionals, and based on local knowledge rather than the "bureaucratic expertise" of representative institutions.

Are all the frames elaborated by the protesters only instrumental? Could it be that regressive aims are masked within a discourse of alternative progress? Stressing the presence of all the mentioned elements in the narratives of the protest does not of course automatically translate into a disconfirmation of the presence of selfish interests, that might be instrumentally hidden behind a more ethical discourse. To a certain extent, the search for "true motives" is difficult to address in empirical social science research focusing on collective frames. However, we have shown that the definition of some fundamental values such as the general good, progress, future or democracy is fundamentally contested. The protest arena is indeed also (sometimes mainly) a space for symbolic struggle over meanings, identities, interests.

In addition the evolution of the conflict, through the interaction of different actors, involves complex shifts in the symbolic scale of the protest. A growth in generality is a symbolic process that facilitates the interactions between different actors. A hypothesis that appears confirmed from our research is that the evolution from a local to a global definition of the conflict, the elaboration of images that show an alternative future and a different conception of the general interest, the conception of these protest actions as a laboratory for an alternative view of politics and a more appropriate definition of democracy all seem to take place in the course of these campaigns. This in fact seems to emerge through the adherence of different actors to the protest (*see* Chap. 2). Committees and local politicians, social centres and trade unions, environmental associations and social forums all meet, network and bridge their more specific frames in the course of the protest. Changes in the symbolic construction of identity, the stakes and the motivations for action all appear to link the protest campaigns in Val di Susa and the Messina Straits with the movement for globalisation from below.

Chapter 4

In Movement: the Repertoires of the Protest

Our main strategy was to raise awareness about the uselessness of the bridge, the tragedy it presented for development, as a tragic example of "not doing" something, of not being concerned with local problems, of another decision that came from above. This was the strategy. It was enacted by informational activities in schools, youth centres, workplace associations, as well as in neighbourhoods and parishes. We were always trying to inform the public and raise a level of awareness [that would make people] capable of mobilisation, ... we did not hide our concern that a crucial moment for the struggle would be to oppose the start of building works. The other strategy was to break the media stranglehold, which was total and terrifying, preventing those outside the area of the Straits from knowing that the people of the Straits did not want the bridge. This was the most difficult thing. (IME 2)

1. Repertoires of Protest: an Introduction

As this activist recalls, in both the Straits and Val di Susa protest campaigns those opposed to the building of these infrastructural projects use a variety of protest strategies in seeking to influence public opinion. Protest is defined in the sociology of social movements as a "resource of the powerless ...[protest forms] depend for success not upon direct utilization of power, but upon activating other groups to enter the political arena" (Lipsky 1965: 1). Protest uses the mass media as indirect channels of participation and allows alliances with more influential actors. In order to obtain a voice, social movements "employ methods of persuasion and coercion which are, more often than not, novel, unorthodox, dramatic and of questionable legitimacy" (Wilson 1973: 227). The same non-conventionality of protest allows those without power to be heard through the channels of the mass media. Large public demonstrations, disruptive direct actions or even symbolically innovative initiatives are those most capable of attracting the attention of public opinion.

Those who protest must also understand the logic in the selection of information by the mass media, and adapt their forms of protest to the characteristics of public institutions. The centralisation of decision-making power during the formation of the nation state led to a repertoire of centralised political activity and social movements organised at the national level (Tilly 1978), while recent challenges to the nation-state have led to the development of multi-level social movement organisations (della Porta and Tarrow 2005). Not only do rational actors mobilise above all when and where they perceive the possibility of success (Tarrow 1994), but their strategies are also influenced by the reaction of the authorities: the opening of channels of access moderates the forms of protest, while their closure easily induces radicalisation (della Porta 1995).

If the protest is a resource that some groups utilise during the decision-making process, it should not be viewed, however, in purely instrumental terms. In fact, protest actions are "sites of contestation in which bodies, symbols, identities, practices and discourse are used to pursue or prevent changes in institutionalized power relations" (Taylor and van Dyke 2004: 268). During the course of a protest both time and money are invested in risky activities; yet often resources of solidarity are also created (or recreated). The protest in fact triggers a sense of collective identity, which is a condition for collective action (Pizzorno 1993). Many forms of protest "have profound effects on the group spirit of their participants", since "in the end there is nothing as productive of solidarity as the experience of merging group purposes with the activities of everyday life" (Rochon 1998: 115; see also Polletta 2006). For workers, strikes and occupations have represented not only instruments for collective pressure but also arenas in which a sense of community is formed (Fantasia 1988) and the same has occurred with the occupation of schools and universities by students (Ortoleva 1988). Furthermore, in social movements the means used are very closely tied to the desired ends: "Tactics represent important routines, emotionally and morally salient in these people's lives" (Jasper 1997: 237).

Contrary to the images of emotional and violent crowds, protests tend to pursue a specific aim through a historically determined path (Tilly 1986: 390). At the same time, however, protest also has a path-dependent evolution, since "the use of standard protest forms also evokes past political movements whose struggles have long since been vindicated as just" (Rochon 1988: 110). In the course of these protest campaigns there is often innovation, as the forms of known protest represent, in the words of Tilly (1986: 390), "a repertoire in something like the theatrical or musical sense of the word; but the repertoire in question resembles that of *commedia dell'arte* or jazz more than that of a strictly classical ensemble: people know the general rules of performance more or less well and vary the performance to meet the purpose at hand".

Taking into account both the instrumental and symbolic value of protest repertoires, we shall look at the protests in Val di Susa and the Messina Straits first as specific forms of communication, observing the role played in each of these by the diffusion of alternative knowledge. In both our cases the initial attention of activists was concentrated on an informational campaign in the territory covered by the two protests (section 2). In addition, both protest campaigns used more disruptive forms of actions: the protesters making their numbers count (section 3); refuting violence, they promoted forms of direct action including the blockage of roads, highways and railway lines, while the sites of the proposed works were either physically occupied (Val di Susa) or symbolically surrounded (Messina) (section 4). In the course of these actions the protesters often met with the police. While raising the possibility that this may delegitimise their protest, the physical struggles became emotionally loaded moments, as the indignation matched the fear of physical consequences and a sense of injustice mobilised the wider community. In the narrative of the activists, during the police charges (as with the site occupations and the camps) the rational cost–benefit analysis of individual actions is superseded by the intrinsic (moral and affective) satisfaction of acting with others, which in turn stimulates processes of mutual recognition. Above all, these campaigns become arenas of interaction between different subjects, with divergent but also convergent views, leading not only to some disputes but also to the creation of new bonds of trust (section 5). Multiple forms of action are therefore used, intertwining and cross-fertilizing the different protest traditions and preferences of the various groups (section 6), while alternative channels of information are both created and exploited (section 7).

2. The Construction of Knowledge

> The people got a real counter-knowledge, and succeeded in defending and then expanding this by building a consensus in the valley, in Turin and in recent months even in Italy as a whole. This work of counter-information took years and years ... and was the real engine of the protest: if you ask an inhabitant of Val di Susa why they are against the Tav, he can talk to you for hours and hours, explaining all the motives for dissent from an environmental and political point of view. (IVS 1)

A widespread belief in both Val di Susa and the Messina Straits is that making people aware of a protest begins through channels of communication. In sociological studies on public policies, communication is identified as central by those who maintain that it is possible to transform a "zero-sum game" on large-scale public works into a "positive-sum game", or at least finding a consensual solution. Studies of transport policies have characterised a very much closed decision-making process, with an important influence of private actors enacted through the control of technical expertise (see, for example, Halpern 2006). According to the hypothesis articulated within the Nimby approach, local conflicts are marked by a difficulty in communicating decisions with a high level of technological content, and by scarce efforts from the promoters of the project to interact with the local population. In this discussion, communication tends to be seen as a unidirectional process, almost an advertising strategy aimed at promoting a product.[1] In our two cases "poor communication" has been admitted by those who support and promote these infrastructural projects.

Adopting a discourse prevalent among scholars of public policy, some pro-Tav actors attribute opposition to the project to a lack of information among the public, for which the former centre-right national government was held responsible. On the eve of the protest of June 2005, the president of the interested region (Piedmont), Mercedes Bresso (Ds), declared that she was aware of the "legitimate concerns of those that inhabit the area", but attributed this to their lack of information: "Faced with the unknown the threat seems much greater. When people are aware whether their home or their land will be within the scope of the project then such protests will diminish. And we shall finally begin to discuss concrete problems" (R 2/11/05). With regard to the Bridge on the Messina Straits, Folco Quilici, the already mentioned documentary film-maker member of the governing board of the company entrusted with realising the project, declared that those who oppose the bridge "do not want it because they don't know what it will be … my aim is exactly to spread this kind of information" (CdS 3/4/05).

The explanation of the conflict as caused by poor communication is rejected by those who protest, who underline their own competences, based on both local and specialist knowledge. In response to Mercedes Bresso, who wants to reassure everyone that "nobody will die", the Mayor of Susa replies: "We are against it precisely because we are well informed" (R 17/11/05). To those who accuse them of poor information, the WWF representative in Messina replies that:

> our principal form of activity has been information, because it allows the citizen involvement in our various events. Information is available through public screenings and the acquisition of data, material and news. We like to have our data at hand, not in abstract form: How many cubic metres of earth will be dug? How many trucks will be used? How much money will be spent? (IME 1)

The availability of technical knowledge has already been identified as a central strategic aim for environmental organisations, which have increasingly sought political and media recognition on the basis of their expertise (della Porta and Diani 2004). In the campaigns against urban pollution, technical information was exploited by citizens' committees and environmental organisations (della Porta 2004a; Lewanski 2004; Piazza 2004). Those who opposed the Tav and the bridge likewise sought detailed technical information on both projects and obtained the advice of specialists. Technical knowledge has the instrumental value of legitimising the opposition. Our two cases allow us to underline that, beyond the role of technical experts (both hired and sympathisers), there is also an interaction between specialist and local knowledge.

Above all in the early phases of the protest, the principal activity of protesters was the collection, elaboration and diffusion of information on the projects, based on technical knowledge obtained through dialogue with experts. In Val di Susa the search for specialist information is evident in the decision of the Mountainous Community to commission a study at Polinomia that could suggest alternative strategies for routing the traffic in the valley, later forming an argument used by No Tav protesters (R 17/8/02).

In the area of the Messina Straits, specialist knowledge is evident in two documents that were highly critical of the "Environmental Impact Study" (SIA – *Studio di Impatto Ambientale*) conducted by the company entrusted with the project ("Straits of Messina – SdM plc"). These documents were presented to the public in February 2003. The first was conducted by various leading environmental organisations (Italia Nostra, Legambiente, WWF) and entitled "The Bridge on the Straits: The study of Straits of Messina plc as an empty shell", and consisted of 250 pages elaborated by a group of experts of various disciplines (www.noponte.org, 19/2/03). The other study was conducted by the Green Party and entitled "10 Good Reasons to Say No", with claims that the SIA should be re-done because it is full of methodological errors and does not apply a strategic environmental evaluation. The project is perceived to be formulated without strategy and planning; it places a brake on the development of shipping, foresees unjustifiable increases in traffic, has elevated public costs and underestimates the ecological impact and the seismic risk (DME 19).

Technical knowledge is not only gained externally but, as with other environmental campaigns (Piazza 2004), can be "internalised" through belonging to a protest of "experts": economists, engineers, urban planners, etc. There are:

> many scholars who have made themselves available to the movement, who have conducted in-depth studies on the work, who have made their own studies available to the population. Also important is the work of the committees, which organised dozens of assemblies, spreading this information around the valley and in Turin. It was important not only to create a generic consensus against the Tav, but also to allow the circulation of information to people so that they become personally involved. (IVS 1)

Interestingly, many technical experts played a key role in initiating the protests against the Bridge on the Messina Straits. The first committee against the project, "Between Scilla and Charybdis", was organised primarily by Calabrian and Sicilian intellectuals and university professors. These included architects, urban planners, geologists, economists, development specialists and transport experts. Their contribution and those of other scholars have been crucial for the development of critical documents and publications with regard to the proposed bridge, focusing not only on its environmental impact (Bettini et al. 2002) but also to its social and cultural impact (Pieroni 2002), as well as for the dissemination of information to the local population.

In general terms, the use of technical information has a legitimising effect on the elaboration and implementation of public policies (Lewanski 2004). Technical "counter-knowledge" is considered a fundamental resource by those who protest: "culture and knowledge, which have always been an instrument of power for the rich, are in this case the instrument of the weak that has rendered him stronger" (IVS 9). It is also potentially useful in order to counter the accusations of "Nimbyism":

> We are accused of a Nimby syndrome among other ridiculous accusations, but in reality we want to address the heart of the matter, because it is only through culture and information that we can win the battle ... we began to inform ourselves from professionals and scholars who live in the territory, who provided their services free of charge in order to study all aspects of this project, from transport to biology. (IVS 7)

Beyond this instrumental use, knowledge can also transform the form and content of the protest. First, the various actors who join in the protest tend to adopt a specialist language. In the No Tav march of June 2003, the thirty-eight mayors that participated recalled they had been expressing their concerns for twelve years about the hydrogeological risks, the possibility that the springs may drain away, the presence of asbestos, which could be dispersed in the air by strong winds (which blow for two-thirds of the year), and epidemiological studies that indicated an already high incidence of tumours (R 1/6/03). Meanwhile, in the area of the Straits, protesters insist that on the basis of existing technical knowledge the bridge will be difficult if not impossible to build (IME 1; IME 4). The committee "Our City of Messina" which organised a popular petition against the bridge in May 2002, underlined the lack of methodological rigour in feasibility studies, the lack of secure foundations due to the seismic risks in the area, the elevated costs, the environmental devastation and the undervaluation of urban problems connected to the project. Besides, the use of knowledge allows for the development of alternative proposals, as for instance in the call for "a complete revision of the general plan of transport ... according to a new and more sustainable conception of transport and mobility", to be realised through "a reduction in vehicle traffic, a reduction in tariffs for the transport of goods and the enhancement of existing infrastructure such as roads, highways and railwaylines" (DME 2).

In the course of the mobilisation, technical knowledge does not remain the preserve of the experts, but becomes appropriated and transmitted by the activists. Indeed a significant part of the activities of organisations opposed to the two public works involves the production, processing and dissemination of information. In the words of one activist, "nights [were] spent watching videos, inserting, archiving, cataloguing and scanning documents, and transforming them into a compatible format" (Margaira 2005: 69). It is precisely through protest that expertise becomes "socialised", communicated in a "lay" form and cross-fertilised with other forms of non-technical knowledge. As one activist puts it: "The public assemblies organised by the 'committees' became evening schools where we learnt what aerodynamic noise pollution was ... that mechanism caused by gear changes, the decibels that increase exponentially" (Sasso 2005: 16). Also the organisations against the bridge underline the central role of information and communication in the mobilising process: "Our principal problem was that of disseminating information, so we set up information kiosks and distributed flyers in the city centre and in northern Messina" (IME 4). This information is often communicated through actions that simulate the damaging effects of these works: in Val di Susa, the reproduction of the noise produced by high-speed trains; in Messina, "in simulation we wound a tape round exactly where they were proposing to build a pylon ... making it evident to people that, should the project go ahead, it would be impossible for them to enter that zone" (IME 3).

Technical knowledge is thus internalised and transformed by activists, who in turn become experts. In fact, those who protest claim to be more knowledgeable than those promoting the works. The widespread belief is that "there are different levels of experts: technical ones, those from the movements, the institutions, and 'normal' people, who can teach themselves with the information gained from different sources" (IVS 5). Technical knowledge is thus combined with local knowledge, which derives from an understanding of the territory. In the words of a mayor from Val di Susa:

> The moment when a legitimate government decides, for the good of the country, to pursue a large-scale public work, I believe that this should be explained to the local population, who retain the right to be informed. In the first place because they know the territory, so from the moment that you intervene heavily in their territory it is wise to hear the opinion of those that inhabit it, because ministers cannot possibly know all these things ... information can also be gained through listening and discussing. (IVS 7)

However, local knowledge should not be seen as "single-issue". It is precisely through this "spreading of knowledge" that different themes are bridged together. Speeches made during union protests, environmental protests, the counter-summit in Genoa, or the European Social Forum allow the diffusion of knowledge with regard to the interested areas, and can lead to the bridging of different themes. In this sense, as in other conflicts, the residents maintain that it is "legitimate to identify and calculate the reasonable risks, not only with regard to technical information, but also on the basis of recognised social values, beyond the freedom of choice, between voluntary and involuntary risks" (Borelli 1999: 33). The conflict therefore regards the founding values of the community, notwithstanding the knowledge of the local context.

3. Protests and the Logic of Numbers

> The first week of mobilisation ended with a magnificent demonstration
> … from Ganzirri to Faro on the Messinese coast, 400–500 people hand
> –in hand up until Torre Faro. It was the moment when we understood
> that it was possible, because through the flyers distributed at the market
> of Giostra [an area of Messina] and discussions with people on the
> Sicilian territory, we understood that there was popular sympathy for
> our ideas and an opposition to the project. (IME 7; also IME 6)

As this activist recalls, the activity of counter-information builds the resources
for mobilisation, preparing the terrain for a protest in the streets. Protest is
normally considered an instrument of voice. Those who lack access to
institutional (or semi-institutional) channels to public power seek to alert public
opinion through protest. As a non-conventional activity, protest ought to attract
the attention of the mass media as it meets the criteria of "newness" (Lipsky
1965). If past research on social movements has highlighted the distortions
introduced by the mass media (Gitlin 1980; Smith et al. 2001), in the last
decades the diffusion of non-conventional forms of action has reduced their
innovative value and thus the likely interest of the press. Becoming ever more
"normal", protests have difficulty in capturing the attention of the media.
Influences can also be exerted on the media by other actors who aim to reduce
coverage or present a distorted image of the protests.

In the case of Val di Susa, an image diffused among the No Tav is that of
mass media strongly hostile to the protest, but whose attention can be captured
through disruptive actions. In the words of one interviewee:

> The established power is too strong: the press, news bulletins have all
> knelt to the Tav, they have always ignored our struggle, at the most
> criminalising it or otherwise stigmatising it as a local struggle led by
> farmers. We sought to offer our best, but were aware that on that level
> it was hard to win. But when it came to the confrontation everyone was
> aware that there was a whole population in the valley that was fighting
> against the high-speed train link. (IVS 1)

In the case of the Messina Straits, the No Bridge activists interviewed agreed in
underlining the hostility of both the local and national media to their protest,
initially expressed by a lack of coverage of their protests and later by almost
unanimously backing the project. There again protests met, according to our
interviewees, a wall of silence:

> We had total censorship for years, speaking to journalists from national
> newspapers that insisted the bridge was inevitable and we must resign

ourselves to it. It was very difficult. Everything went through the Internet for years. Then with the protest on 8 December 2004 we managed to tear down this wall and appeared in twenty national newspapers; then there were interviews with papers from America, England, Germany, Spain, France. (IME 1)

Disruptive protest appears here to be instrumental in attracting the attention of a collusive or distracted media. An activist recalls that:

in the months of September and October a postal account was set up, entitled "One euro for the valley", with the scope of raising a national profile that the media were not concerned with or only in a partial manner. The aim was to buy pages of newspaper to raise awareness of the truth. After 31 October we no longer needed this as the media came to us, the movement suddenly became "important" and there was a massive concentration of journalists, both those concerned with honest coverage and those seeking to write partisan or incomplete reportages. (IVS 7)

In the same vein, research on social movements has underlined the relevance of the "logic of numbers". Numbers become a sort of substitute election, demonstrations having much more audience (and later success) the larger they are. In our two cases the growth in participation rates was seen by activists as a sign of growing consensus for their actions. The logic of numbers also has an effect on the mass media, increasing the visibility and demonstrating a growing consensus and legitimisation around the protest.

With regard to Val di Susa, this "logic of numbers" is underlined in the words of an interviewee who defines participation in protests as an indication of the support of the population, and therefore the likely prospects of success:

The first crucial step was in 2003, the Borgone–Bussoleno protest … this was very important for understanding if the local population was in our favour, or if they were indifferent or resigned, which was our main fear (other protests occurred from 1996 to 2003 but were not well attended) … this key protest in 2003 saw 20,000 people participate and people became aware that the battle could indeed be won. (IVS 4)

With regard to the Messina Straits, the progressive numerical increase in participation at the rallies, which from 2002 onwards led the mobilisation against the bridge, was underlined by our interviewees: "The rallies began with 400 to 500 people in 2002, but later became mass rallies with thousands participating" (IME 5). The growth in participation has not only instrumental effects, but also symbolic ones, becoming a symbol of how well rooted within the local community this protest had become.

4. Direct Action and Solidarity

The deputy police commissioner glimpsed local politicians: my councillor and I were wearing the national flag; it was not the first time that the state turned on itself, but this time it was strange because it was the deputy commissioner that gave me orders to evacuate the streets in 5 minutes. They would have passed through anyway! At this point I began to call other politicians, various other people, asking them to come and join us. We are fortunate that we know the mountains well, the paths and mule tracks. After 10 minutes the deputy commissioner returned to ask us what we had decided, and I replied that we would not move and would defend our territory. At this point the police advanced with their shields above their heads. We conducted an entirely pacific resistance, with our hands in the air; we were retreating because we could not stand such a conflict, until behind us came reinforcements from everywhere, which helped us to resist the advance. So many people arrived that the police had to stop, and despite pushing us aside, they were unable to move us. This went on until late in the evening, it was a very tough confrontation, from 7 in the morning till 8 in the evening; until the deputy commissioner, in agreement with the President of the Mountainous Community, suspended their activities. At that point we decided to leave, as the police themselves were doing. That same night the police occupied the area. (IVS 7)

This is the chronicle of one of the transforming events of the protest in Val di Susa, the Battle of Seghino on 31 October 2006 according to the mayor of a town in Val di Susa. Often in line with an increase in the number of protesters there is a propensity for more disruptive actions, as more moderate actions have been attempted but are seen as ineffective against the perceived "brick wall" of the authorities (della Porta and Mosca 2007). In the protest against the construction of large infrastructures (incinerators, airports, etc.), the phase of mass demonstrations is often accompanied by direct actions such as blocking roads or railway lines, which despite excluding violence represent anyway a challenge to the state in terms of public order. A radicalisation of conflict is particularly evident in Val di Susa, around a classic mechanism of interaction with the police, which also attains a symbolic value. There is here an escalation in the physical conflicts, centred around the occupation of the building site, which both sides are seeking to control.

The Battle of Seghino; police charges in Venaus on 29 November; the dispersal of the site occupation on 6 December; the reoccupation of the site on 8 December: these are the most acute moments of conflict with the police, phases of an escalation that accompanied waves of mobilisation. In sociological studies, the effectiveness of protest is tied to the ability to interrupt routine, often through non-conventional acts. Public order is often a central frame for those who oppose the protest, and ours are no exception to this rule. Above all from the second half of 2005, the No Tav protesters are accused by Tav supporters of being not only selfish, but also violent. The rationale for clearing out the site of Seghino on the night of December 5th–6th was, according to the then Minister of the Interior, "to revert to minimal conditions of legality and to relaunch dialogue" by "blocking the extremist fringe before it affected Turin and the Winter Olympics" (R 16/12/05). Similar views were held among the centre-left coalition, with the Piedmontese Secretary of the Democrats of the Left (DS) asserting that "there is an ever-increasing risk of a degenerating situation while the threat of a possible terrorist act grows daily" (R 6/11/05).

Despite the risk of stigmatisation, direct action is perceived by those who oppose these two projects as an instrument that raises the visibility of a protest ignored by the mass media. As the President of the Mountainous Community recalls:

> Thanks to Minister Pisanu our visibility increased. I was hoping that this would happen, because from an electoral viewpoint 100,000 people count for nothing (given that they all vote differently), but if the protest spreads throughout Italy then their fear grows and their insults escalate along with the accusations of "localism". For this reason we are talking of a "large backyard"'. (IVS 8)

The activists' perception is that, even beyond the valley, "the attacks by the police earned the sympathy of those who knew nothing of the Tav … for them it was counterproductive because it gave us added visibility and prompted a democratic spirit that went beyond the Tav conflict, because in a democratic country certain things should not be done" (IVS 3).

Beyond the instrumental dimension linked to increased visibility, activists underline however also the positive effects of direct action as a moment of growth in solidarity with the local population. It is precisely the effect of the injustice frame (Gamson 1990) that is often mentioned by protesters as a source of consensus within the community and a mechanism that reinforces identification. The intervention of the police in the site occupation became the symbol of an unfair attitude towards those who were protesting peacefully, the military occupation of the area "being seen as an arrogance that nobody could justify" (IVS 4). As a local inhabitant observes, "the explosion of the movement (and nobody expected a participation of this strength) occurred from 31 October onwards, the days in which the violence of the government sent the troops into the valley" (IVS 2). However, the charges in Seghino represent, in the narrative of the protest, a moment of mobilisation that goes beyond mere external solidarity, helping the development of a sense of a "struggling community". In the words of an activist, "At the site occupation there were always 100–200 people during the day. When it looked likely to be cleared out then 2,000–3,000 people arrived, staying throughout the night to defend our position" (IVS 11).

Participation becomes more intense when faced with a perceived external aggression, described by activists as an act of war against a peaceful community. In the words of one activist, the perceived police intrusion forces the community to "join the front –line":

> People appeared in very large numbers on a week day; they didn't go to work but went to the site occupation instead, believing that there was no use in just talking but that they should join the front line. They all appeared with banners and flags. In Bruzolo, when the police were confronting the crowd, we joined in with our household utensils to defend ourselves. We are not afraid of anybody; we want to defend our territory in a peaceful way. Maybe you will laugh at us, but the battle is long. (IVS 5)

Injustice, arrogance and dislike are the principal narrative frames that emerge with regard to the presence of the police on the territory, perceived as a "militarisation of the valley". Its consequences are often recalled as an act of violence on the territory and its inhabitants. The personalisation of the narrative through direct experiences communicates a sentiment of indignation:

> On the night of the 29th my mobile rang. It was a friend of mine who said that they had come out and militarised the area. I set out with my heart in my mouth, the news made me feel trodden on and tricked, with respect to a struggle that we had always conducted in the open, without subterfuge, while they carried out their actions in the middle of the night ... at Venaus they would not let anyone enter, we were stopped by the riot police. The scenes I witnessed were truly shocking; lots of people that normally start work at dawn could not enter. An old woman arrived saying that she had to look after her granddaughter and the police told her to have the baby taken out of the town, as she would not be able to get in. (IVS 4)

In the core narrative of the protest the militarisation of the valley is the "final drop that makes the glass spill over", while the subsequent mobilisation is the "reaction against arrogance: the moment in which they made false moves with arrogance and even trickery there was a popular reaction, from everybody, not just militants" (IVS 4). In the perception of the activists it is from this moment that:

> the people started to get angry. There was no way of stopping them; they occupied roads and the highways (the people, not the associations), they would have stayed day and night until the government gave a signal ... from 1 November till 6 December it went ahead like this, then on the 6th they used force, beating old people.

Two days later people shouted "let's take back the land" and 100,000 people descended and took it back. (IVS 5)

In this way, the narrative provides a sense of the causes-effects relationship between the repression and mobilisation of the community.

The same indignation emerges in the narratives on the dispersal of the site occupation by the police forces, where the injustices perpetrated against the young and the old are framed as an attack against a community, whose courage is stressed as testified to by the very history of the valley. In the recollection of one activist:

> they destroyed the books of the university students who were studying (after all this was time taken away from daily activities), throwing them in a bonfire. And, when people were forced to leave the fields, the police went round with the No Tav banners as if they were a symbol of conquest …. and they also had the cheek to destroy the food supplies that were needed to live in the camp … old people were beaten and they stopped the ambulances from coming. An old man stayed an hour slumped on the ground, because they never even let the stretchers in. (IVS 10)

On the same line, there is a frequent recollection of "a police chief on a caterpillar truck shouting on a megaphone 'Crush them all!' and encouraging the driver to push ahead until it was right in front, a nasty and dangerous experience that I will remember all my life because it was the first time I was scared that something awful could happen" (IVS 4).

Indignation against a perceived arrogance of the state is what emerges from these interviews and lies at the root of the growth of the movement, affecting its capacity to react. If repression increases the costs of collective action it can often have the effect of discouraging it. However, it may also reinforce the processes of identification and solidarity (della Porta and Reiter 2006). On 31 October, the reconquest of Seghino (the place where the works were due to begin) is narrated as an epic return with intense feelings of joy. In the words of one interviewee, the police charges mark the start of:

> the time of fighting: the morning after in the valley there was a massive strike. The workers left their factories, the teachers never entered the schools while the parents never took their children there, and everyone went to occupy the valley, which remained so for three days. It was the time of the revolt, which culminated on 8 December with the reconquest of the field. It was wonderful. (IVS 10)

The memories of the police blockade at Mompatero are added to the observation that "even the meek people in front of injustice are capable of rebellion and will not turn back, because they understand it is a question of pride and dignity. This was the most important thing" (ibid.).

Even if the frame of violence is rarely used by proponents of the Bridge on the Messina Straits, where building works have not begun, it is predicted that there "will still be problems because non-violent direct action will be savagely repressed, especially if they should start the building works" (IME 5).

5. Protest as an Arena: Site Occupations and Camps

> Our identity started to strengthen from June, when the government tried to initiate the works. That summer people began to stay at the occupied sites from morning till night, people from the same town who were only acquaintances before now became friends. The pensioners said that we should "do it in this way because the battle is not over", because they understood the difference between watching it on TV and organising activities. The people became a community … the site occupation became a social event and this cemented an identification between territory and citizen that is quite exceptional. Then the events of Venaus obviously emphasised the solidarity in these difficult situations. People ended up in hospital from police beatings, and a sense of community had been created. (IVS 8)

As emerges from this interview with the President of the Mountainous Community of Lower Val di Susa, the 'militarisation' of the area and the police charges were perceived by activists as something that legitimised their protest through a feeling of indignation. The "people" became a "community" through long and intense actions, such as the site occupation or the campsites, which affected the daily lives of the participants and formed arenas of communication and (often tense) discussions between its various political and territorial components.

In the case of Val di Susa, the struggles around the No Tav site occupation of 2005 were seen as a moment of growth for the protest not only in numerical terms, but also in terms of identification with the protest. In the words of activists, the site occupation had "great emotional force", producing "a shared intimacy", it was "wonderful as well as striking for the behaviour of the people, the diversity of those present, and the sense of serenity" (Sasso 2005: 61). In the memory of the activists, there are the "unforgettable nights of Venaus, when we had a bonfire in the fields and the snow fell, and we felt truly united" (Velleità Alternative 2006: 20). In the narrative of the activists the site occupation is remembered as a serene but intense experience that reinforced feelings of mutual trust:

> When on the night of 5–6 December the police forces went to occupy the land at Venaus … there was a wonderful encampment under the

falling snow, fires burning, children and dogs playing. There were pots full of food, young people from all over Italy – because at that point we became the focus and hope for a series of struggles. All this they stopped with batons, beatings and by destroying our tents. (IVS 10)

These site occupations are in fact seen as places of strong socialisation, "real homes built on this territory, which became focal points – a wonderful thing. In the summer there were scores of people that came to talk and socialise, allowing feelings of solidarity to grow with the awareness that this struggle was for everyone" (IVS 11). Participation in the protest was seen as gratifying in itself, affecting daily life: "Throughout the whole summer there were 50–100 people that occupied three places in the valley (Borgone, Bruzolo, Venaus). In the morning, you went to get a coffee at the site occupation and not at the bar. If you wanted an alternative dinner you went to the site occupation, where you might also *see* a concert" (IVS 5).

Allowing frequent and emotionally intense interactions, the site occupations were perceived as an opportunity for reciprocal identification, based on mutual recognition as members of a community. Accordingly, in the activists' memory, "this is the story of an unwitting revolution, as a young man said, in these days we also changed, lost our prejudices and struck up friendships. People met each other that previously would have had little occasion to ... we met, listened and found that we shared a common destiny" (Sasso 2005: 62–63). In the site occupations, "you got to know people through the struggle, you recognized each other" (IVS 10) The action itself is so seen as an occasion for creating and strengthening resources of mutual solidarity and reciprocal trust, which allows to withstand later moments of intense conflict.

These site occupations therefore represent arenas of discussion and deliberation, places to experiment with a different form of democracy, participatory because it allows for the deployment of individual creativity. In the words of one activist: "Everything began from these site occupations, a wonderful form of participatory democracy where people from below could have their say: they could coin a slogan, a new banner, invent a new march, a new message" (IVS 5). The site occupations thus become "political laboratories" that produced intense interactions and communication:

Unity is so strong in the No Tav movement, we are so compact that we always overcome the many obstacles we have to face ... for us militants, this struggle was a political laboratory, a moment of incredible growth, because very often it is difficult to act concretely... we utter beautiful words on the world we want, the contradictions we want to eliminate. Here we threw ourselves into the game, we experimented on the things we said and we learnt a lot from these people, from their motivation, their capacities. And we had to confront the realities of our own words, which were far from the realities of political action. We concretised ourselves in a struggle of this type, and it was a moment of growth (both human and political) for all of us. (IVS 1)

The experience of the site occupations therefore transcends the opposition to high-speed trains; they became the places in that "all the small problems which must be confronted daily are resolved through discussion, with spontaneous assemblies, with mutual trust and a complicity that reinforces the sense of solidarity" (ibid.). New values, for example "the absence of money" (Velleità Alternative 2006: 134), were experimented with in everyday life. In the words of one activist:

> The site occupations were places inhabited by a different kind of life, where you could eat for free because money no longer had any value, and this not only attracted people like myself, who have a vision of this that is not only an ideal. I believe that this reality can be implemented; I believe in the possibility of radically changing this world and not only reforming it … it was a collective hope and when they responded with militarisation the people rebelled. (IVS 10)

A similar but distinct role in the construction of alternative arenas of communication and discussion is played by the "campsite of struggle", present in both mobilisations. Above all in the No Bridge campaign, the campsites on both sides of the Straits performed and helped the development of the protest campaign, as well as affecting the dynamics of cooperation and conflict between the various political and territorial actors, particularly in the phase preceding the mass demonstrations. These camps facilitated contacts between activists and organisations, furthering the process of cross-issue networking, particularly with regard to large-scale public works. This extension in the aims of mobilisation is highlighted by participants at the campsites, who note the:

> consolidation and amplification of networks, and the coordination of movements that challenge those who wish to degrade our social, environmental and territorial quality of life, through large-scale public works and other operations that seek to use the places and spaces of our lives to serve the interests of monopolistic capital and speculators. It is particularly useful to extend this protest to the committees that more generally oppose large-scale public works and related issues, while connecting it with the environmental and cultural organisations, improving also the exchange of information, news and resources between groups active in these local realities. (DME 23)

If the campsites on both sides of the Straits are located within a broader global movement for social justice (the first international campsite was on the agenda proposed at the European Social Forum in Florence 2002), a multi-issues discourse is amplified during the protest campaign.

While representing arenas of discussion and communication that favour processes of networking, dialogue and collaboration between different political (both moderate and radical) and territorial (Messina and Calabria) groups, the campsites remain distinct from the building site occupations described above, in that they only represented part of a larger movement. A journalist-activist we interviewed observes that, while collaboration is evident, so is territorial competition between the two sides of the Straits:

> The campsite of 2002 was the first moment in which the two souls of the movement, that from Messina and that from Calabria, which have always had difficulty working and developing together, had a moment of synthesis and mutual recognition (hitherto they only knew each other from Internet blogs or emails). They dialogued and worked together. Bear in mind that other camps (in 2003, 2004) saw conflicts along geographical rather than political lines. This led to a separation into two different camps located in two different places with their different agendas. (IME 5)

The continual tension between unity of action and ideological diversity is confirmed by a Calabrian activist from the "antagonistic" component, made of squatted social centres and autonomous organisations. On the one hand, the evolution of the campsite on both sides of the Straits is seen as an example of an "inclusive dynamic":

> In 2002 the proposals of some comrades to develop links with the Calabrian side in the direction of inclusive dynamic was fully received, and so some of us Calabrians participated in the campsite on the Sicilian coast, while others organised joint initiatives on the Calabrian coast; connecting the two sides of the Straits in a joint struggle was a winning tactic. (IME 7)

On the other hand, tensions emerged already during the first campsite, linked to prior organisational identities and their competition.

Leaving aside these tensions and internal divisions, the campsites were important moments for debates on various themes beyond those more closely tied to the question of the bridge. They allowed the formulation of alternative proposals and new strategies of protest activity, such as holding open seminars, workshops and plenary assemblies.[2] As can be read from one of the concluding documents:

> The plenary assemblies, which contributed towards deepening our scientific, technical and political knowledge on many themes, also proposed scenarios for sustainable development of the territory, presenting an alternative to the failed model of development adopted in Southern Italy. In this sense we pledged to maintain and develop a wider movement of ideas, proposals, knowledge, conflict, rebellion, capable of confronting the devastation and misery caused by the prevailing capitalist model of development. (DME 23)

Also the interviewees noted their own increased political awareness and their capacity for theoretical elaboration. Above all, daily and face-to-face interactions create "human and political" relationships: "The campsites have been moments of internal political growth for the activists, because they are occasions for analyses, elaborations, human and political relations", among other ways through the production, during the second campsite, of a document ("Stop the development of capital") "that was of great political value, regarding not only the bridge but also the complex contradictions of the Italian South" (IME 5).

In addition, the interviewees noted that the campsites were also instruments to raise awareness, involve and potentially mobilise the local population through numerous initiatives on the territory, demonstrations and continual interaction with the surrounding realities. About the campsite in summer 2003, the activists underlined:

> the positive communication between the participants of the campsite and the local population at Villa, Cannitello and Messina; the solidarity shown by the people from Gazzi in Messina during the march around the prison; the impressive adherence to the march in Messina on 1 August and at Villa San Giovanni on the 2nd. These elements demonstrate that it is possible to wake the local population from their slumber despite Mafia threats and a powerfully distorted media campaign. (DME 23)

6. Multiform Action

Until now we have used instruments of political pressure (demonstrations, debates, appeals, etc.); scientific and technical instruments (publications, seminars, research); judicial acts (legal recourses and appeals); informational campaigns to raise awareness (flyers, press conferences, exhibitions, etc.). We believe that the time has now come to use economic instruments in the No Bridge campaign, a non-violent method that has been used for many years in various movements across the world, in order to oppose the producers and retailers of instruments of death and to oppose the power of the multinationals, the economic corporations that violate our human, social, economic and political rights. (DME 22)

This document of the No Bridge protesters refers to the broad and diverse repertoire of collective action that frequently characterises protest campaigns (della Porta and Rucht 2002). During the course of the No Tav and No Bridge campaigns, an already plural repertoire of action became enriched by the interaction with the movement for globalisation from below, already characterised by its adoption of innovating and diverse tactics. The social and political heterogeneity of the movement led to the crossfertilisation of different repertoires: the diverse organisations against neoliberal globalisation used a heterogeneous repertoire of action, shaping and adapting the forms of action developed in the past by different movements that converged within it (della Porta 2003b: 65–67).

Our two campaigns are, at least in part, embedded in this movement; their activists repeatedly underline the heterogeneity and complementarity of the various forms of protest adopted, all peaceful and rigorously non-violent. In the course of the protest against the Bridge, beyond the counter-informational initiatives, the campsites and the mass demonstrations, we also *see* legal actions developed at national and European level, as well as high-impact symbolic acts to attract media attention, such as the crossing of the Straits by "marine cyclists" in July 2002, the demonstration via ferry between Messina and Villa San Giovanni in August 2003, the "non-stop oratorical marathon" and the nautical demonstration "wave upon wave" in the summer of 2005. Similarly, while No Tav activists frequently made appeals to national courts and to the European Commission, they also organised initiatives with a high symbolic impact and visibility, such as theatre performances, films, concerts or even giant No Tav banners located in the most visible (and often difficult to reach) places on the top of the mountains.

In more general terms, the protest marches hold a symbolic importance, both as a direct testimony of involvement and as an expression of territorial rootedness. According to an interviewee from Val di Susa, "there are some folkloristic-cultural features of the movement that are very beautiful. Our demonstrations always end in parties and music, when we don't end up fighting [the police]! We celebrated the New Year in Venaus, thousands of people came to stay in the cold instead of doing normal things; there is also this dimension" (IVS 3). Even in the Straits:

> There were some symbolic initiatives, banners, flyers; there was a nice symbolic initiative in which we handed the Mayors of Messina and Villa San Giovanni a placard with our ideas on what constitutes development in the area of the Straits, and more generally in Sicily and Calabria, contrasting it with what the bridge proposes. It was also a dynamic demonstration. From Villa we took a ferry with the sea

transport workers. This summer [2005] there was the procession of the boats in the Straits ... we also conduct our protest in this folkloristic and theatrical way, which guarantees visibility while contrasting with the flat Pro Bridge campaign, which has no critical capacity. (IME 4)

The repertoire of action is enriched during the course of the two campaigns. The different nodes of the protest network (*see* Chapter 2) in fact bring different forms of action. For example, the patrimony of judicial actions is a feature of environmental associations. In the campaign against the bridge:

Beyond informational initiatives, another thing done by the various environmental associations was to contest the project through legal means, recourse to the appeal court, the Council of State (done in June 2005), denunciations to the Public Prosecutor, to the European Union, for violating Community Directives and the Objective Law ... These are all parallel actions, because the battle is over 360 degrees, in order to convince the politicians that the bridge is useless, to inform people, to send out communications, to react to all the nonsense that they say about us, to organise new forms of protest. (IME 1)

In Val di Susa, beyond the educational initiatives, Habitat was also involved in legal actions, beginning with a demand for a copy of the technical-administrative documents of the project in 1992. In both campaigns referendums are proposed in order to allow the populations involved to express their view, "above all because, through a popular consultation, there is a possibility to expand the informational campaign" (DME 18).

In both campaigns the squatted social centres bring their experience of direct actions, the mayors bring their institutional repertoires of action, the pacifists their fasts and the priests their vigils. The forms of protest are thus "imported" from the experience of other movements, through the multiple belonging of activists. For example, the most recent phase of the campaign saw the use of the boycott, a form of protest often used by the movement for globalisation from below (della Porta 2003b). Already in 2001 the activists promoted boycotts of banks that financed the Tav project in Val di Susa (Sasso 2005: 45), and later they did the same for the Winter Olympics. In the No Bridge campaign, the protestors boycotted banks, businesses and insurance companies involved in the bridge project. In launching a National Boycott Campaign against the Bridge (March 2006), the promoters are not only aware of the plural forms of action already adopted, but also underline the need to invent new and more incisive practices:

We propose to the citizens, political and social groups, unions, associations involved in defending the territory and the environment to boycott those businesses, banks and insurance companies that have decided to directly and indirectly support the realisation of the Bridge on the Messina Straits ... the Boycott Campaign against the Bridge will be launched with a letter to the banks and insurance companies that control shares in the construction companies that form the conglomerate of the General Contractor for the Bridge (Impregilo, Società Italiana Condotte, CMC Cooperativa Muratori Cementisti). In addition we shall boycott Benetton products, as this is the holding company of Impregilo, and Autogrill, controlled by the same group from Treviso. (DME 22)

In the course of protest the repertoires of action expand therefore, with the pragmatic use of varied forms of action, coming from the different traditions of the various actors that participate in the campaign.

7. Protest and Communication

Websites, mailing lists, widely accessed forums were set up; in our site we had links to all the other sites involved with the Tav; Indymedia, despite its limits, was used to circulate information and notices. Even here the committees understood the utility of this medium and were able to exploit it, although with differing levels of ability. On the one hand technology is useful, on the other hand it can be destructive; when you have your own medium and you are aware of how it works, fine, but if you have to use the medium of others then developing a discourse is difficult: many of us were unprepared for this aspect. (IVS 1)

In both Val di Susa and the Straits many initiatives were conceived and realised with the aim of attracting attention from the media. However, the activists remained concerned about the type of message conveyed by these different forms of action and how to influence it. In particular:

When images of the confrontation were diffused, the movement was capable of exploiting this media spotlight, in order to shape the analysis of these events ... The ability to use the media is a reality we must confront, we are not those that break the cameras of journalists or refuse to speak with them, in fact we try to use the chance to transform the coverage. (IVS 1)

As with this interviewee, many activists underline the need to go beyond the concept of the protest as "news" and to develop autonomous resources of communication within the movement. With regard to the mass media, while their relevance is certainly recognised, so also is the danger of distortion of the message and even the structure of the movement. On the one hand, the activists point to the tendency of the press to make spectacles out of events, with an emphasis only on the most radical actions, often criminalising the protest. According to the President of the Mountainous Community:

> We have entered into a position of overexposure in the media, with journalists looking to depict the picturesque, the unrehearsed, and then we are all labelled in the same way. The Olympic flame, which we asked not to stop, passed through more easily here than in other regions but this was enough to criminalise us ... I had proposed not to block it, precisely to get coverage ... when there were tensions the cameramen were there almost encouraging us to do something to get coverage. (IVS 8)

On the other hand, the mass media tend to personalise the message, searching for and creating "media leaders". In Val di Susa, "in part the media worked within the movement, in part they turned it into folklore, building media leaders (choosing people that fitted the profile) and so on" (IVS 2).

The awareness that a media product is the result of interaction between various subjects, and that it can be influenced by these, has led social movements to create autonomous media, which develop above all in the moments of greatest mobilisation (Downing 2001). New technologies are perceived as important instruments for a communication from below. In Val di Susa, "The Internet was a real and proper instrument of information and aggregation for the struggle: the volunteers managed the site, uploaded the documents, maintained contact with the outside world" (IVS 3). The Internet was also widely used by the No Bridge activists and organisations. At least eight websites were openly in favour of the No Bridge campaign (cariddiscilla.it, messinasenzaponte.it, messinasocialforum.it, noponte.org, nopontestrettomessina.it, pontopoli.it, retenoponte.org, terrelibere.org).

In both our cases, websites mainly perform logistical-organisational as well as cognitive-informational functions, in addition to symbolic, protest and advocatory ones (della Porta and Mosca 2006). In order to spread information not covered by the mass media, "ad hoc sites were born, historic sites were amplified, all managed by activists: ours is a movement composed of skilled people" (IVS 7). The Internet is seen as fundamental to guaranteeing internal communication between the various actors present in the valley. According to a widespread opinion, new technologies were "very useful because in real time we managed to send, through mobile phones and digital cameras, videos throughout the world" (IVS 5). The Internet permits the functioning of what an activist describes as the "organised disorganisation" of the movement:

> There is a noticeboard on the Internet (the two sites of reference are Legambiente Val Susa and No Tav) that allows you to *see* what is happening where, and then later via SMS ... On the night of the 6th, in about two hours more than 1,000 people got together. At the first charge of the police (around 23:00) all the mayors were present together with 5,000 people. (IVS 5)

The mobilisation spreads rapidly via "chain SMS". But new technologies also facilitate contacts beyond the valley. As an interviewee puts it, "we hope that national public opinion wakes up; in these days there are people from all over Italy (No Mose, No Bridge, Mugello), many associations and communes from all over Italy; we receive around 100–200 emails every day from people, Italian or European, that want to join this No campaign against the waste of resources" (IVS 5).

The positive effects of the Internet are most evident when face-to-face relationships have been established beforehand (della Porta and Mosca 2006). There is in fact the acknowledgement of an evident risk from exclusively virtual communication:

> I think that sometimes this kind of progress can kill the movement, because you give the impression to your comrades that by sending an email you have done something, that is, you replace human contact with the virtual life and militancy. Where there were also human relations, then it worked well, because the Internet was an instrument for fast communication. It allowed us to work with great speed: Not using technology as a substitute but as a means for integration was very useful. (IVS 2)

Despite its wide use, our interviewees also highlight the limits of the Internet for communicating with the outside world, particularly those not mobilised in the protest:

> The movement uses the Internet a lot. The website is a very useful channel, above all for staying in touch with other subjects of the movement; it has more internal than external capacities. An example is the wonderful work done by Indymedia and Radio Black Out of Turin on the issues in Val di Susa, which we can *see* live; but it is always we activists that use it to communicate between ourselves. (IME 4)

In conclusion, activists do not rely exclusively on the mass media to report upon their disruptive actions, as the the Internet has amplified the resources for communication. However, the shift from internal to external communication remains difficult, as the latter remains permeated by the logic of the mass media, which activists cannot control and whose potential dangers they clearly recognise.

8. Concluding Remarks

The repertoires of protest in both the Messina Straits and Val di Susa are multiple and varied, embracing almost the whole spectrum of forms for protest action, from the more moderate to the more radical, but always non-violent. These range from direct action to procedural acts, from mass demonstrations to symbolic initiatives.

Information and counter-information based on a solid technical-scientific understanding play a fundamental role in both campaigns and are considered by some to be the "principal form of action" (IME 1), above all in the early phases of the protest. The counter-knowledge provided by technical experts serves not only to criticise the projects but also to develop alternatives that become internalised within the movement, both through the participation of experts in the campaign (defined as "cultural fathers of the movement" in the Straits), as well as through diffusion to the activists and citizens involved in the protests. Technical knowledge has a legitimising function and shapes the features of the movement in both our cases, while crossfertilising with local knowledge and other themes.

During the protest campaign there is an increase in forms of demonstrative action. The importance of the "logic of numbers" becomes evident with the participation of the local population in both cases. High adherence is seen as a sign of growing consensus for protest action and plays a legitimising function, in addition to raising visibility in the media and with public opinion. When the "logic of numbers" is combined with direct actions (blockades, occupation of the building site), and when these are repressed by the police (as in Val di Susa), there is the image spreads of a growing internal and external solidarity for the movement. It is precisely this sense of injustice that allows the emergence of consensus inside the community and the movement, as well as winning the sympathy of both public opinion and associations beyond the valley.

The protest is also an arena, a place where different actors meet, communicate and confront, although sometimes tensions emerge. As with the occupation of factories in the labour movement, the site occupations (above all in Val di Susa) have a long duration and are territorially rooted, creating a communitarian identity through reciprocal identification and the belief that they are experimenting with new values and practices of participatory democracy. Though limited temporally, the campsites (especially those on the two sides of the Straits) play an important role in the construction of the campaign: they favour the intensification and expansion of cross-issue networking processes between activists from different groups; they represent important moments of debate that allow the formulation of proposals and strategies for action; they become instruments to raise awareness and to mobilise the local population, interacting with the surrounding territorial reality; and they allow the different strands of the protest to meet and work together despite moments of tension.

The forms of protest in our two cases are varied, both instrumental and symbolic, procedural and countercultural. The various nodes in the protest network bring their own repertoire of actions (legal actions by environmental organisations; strikes by workers; direct actions by the social centres; institutional pressures exerted by the mayors). In this process of diffusion, various forms of action are imported from contemporary movements (e.g. boycotting certain goods, typical in movements for globalisation from below). This same variety of forms is itself claimed as a sign of support and involvement.

Despite these common traits, some differences also emerge between the two campaigns, above all from the impact of direct actions (in particular, the site occupations) and the varying dynamics connected with these. This can be linked to the different "windows of opportunity" presented in the No Tav and the No Bridge campaigns. The fear of immediate dangers certainly pushed the No Tav movement to choose direct action, and to find support for it, whereas in the Straits building work has not begun.

An analysis of the repertoires of protest confirms the innovative features of these campaigns, which are not limited to known forms of action – the repertoire that Tilly (1978) observes – but become intertwined and innovative, in a process of crossfertilisation in action. In certain moments of this process the resources invested in the action multiply. As Alessandro Pizzorno (1997) observes with regard to the movements of the 1960s and 1970s, the resources of militancy become produced and reproduced in the phase of expansion of the protest, when the opportunity for action reduces internal conflict. It is instead during the lulls of mobilisation that we may witness more "competition for scarce resources" among the protesting groups. Especially in these moments, the traditional strategic dilemmas between moderate action, which attracts broader sympathies, and more radical forms, which tend to strengthen internal solidarity, are more acutely felt. The challenge is here not only taking away old boundaries, as instruments to enlarge mobilisation, but also to reconstructing boundaries that go beyond the community (D'Arcus 2006).

Notes

1. On this asymmetric conception of information, *see* Borelli 1999: 49.
2. During the 2003 campsite seminars were held on "Environmental Protection and the Territorial Management of Fundamental Resources"; "Bridges Between People – the Mediterranean, Immigration and Cooperation"; "Local Projects and Alternative Production"; "The Politics of Large-Scale Public Works and Imperialism – What Space for the Movement?' (www.noponte.org). In the course of the third meeting in July 2004 against the Bridge on the Messina Straits organised by the Messina Social Forum at Torre Faro (Messina), seminars were organised on such different themes as international voluntary work; fair trade and critical consumption; the demilitarisation of Sicily; the new municipalism and participatory democracy; the Mafia and large-scale public works; the abolition of the Centre for the Temporary Internment of Undocumented Migrants (www.terrelibere.org).

Chapter 5

Voices of the Valley, Voices of the Straits: a Conclusion

They are trying to stop this formidable resistance, accusing us of being conservative, backward, enemies of progress. They try to isolate each of these protests by defining them as "not in my backyard". But the local dimension of these struggles immediately raises global questions, which in the case of the Tav is a criticism against the realisation of large European infrastructure networks, which consider territory as simply a space to cross, a resource to exploit and violate ... or, in the case of the Bridge on the Straits, we are redefining the concept of what constitutes "development" in the South and its relationship with the people and cultures of the Mediterranean area.

We oppose large-scale public works not for localistic reasons, but in order to defend the territory as a precious common good for everyone, not even just the community that resides in it. Therefore the defence of a territory, its history, its identity, its quality of life, the fabric of social relations that have grown on it, is transformed here into a series of claims (both local and global) that bring about a radical criticism of a model of development that is decided elsewhere, by strong and opaque powers, in the name of the superior interest of profit and the exploitation of common goods. (DME 27)

This extract from a report produced by the National Assembly against Large-scale Public Works summarises the key arguments of the mobilised groups, mentioning (both implicitly and explicitly) the interpretative schemes of the conflict against large-scale public works that we presented in the introductory chapter. At the end of our research we should return to these interpretations, discussing them in particular from a comparative perspective.

Studies of earlier conflicts over the construction of high-impact infrastructural projects have tended to consider the interests, values and preferences of actors as being exogenous to the conflict, characterising them either as egotistic Nimby protests or as social conflicts related to the competing conceptions of the territory, as linked to its values of use or values of exchange. Our perspective here has been to focus on how the actors themselves define their interests, values and preferences. These definitions evolve through a symbolic struggle over identity, motivations for action, and a definition of what is at stake.

The Nimby interpretation of local conflict is contradicted in our cases by the definition the actors themselves provide for their actions, the networked organisation of the conflict, which includes many non-local actors, and the reach of the protest, which involves multiple territorial levels of governance. The report cited above is one of many sources that links different protests accused of the Nimby syndrome (such as No Tav and No Bridge) to a common theme. While an appeal to the community is made, which underlines the natural and social particularities of the area, the vision projected of territory is increasingly open in both protests. Geographical analyses of other territorial conflicts have confirmed that the image of space influences the symbolic construction of conflict, as historical experience determines whether space is defined in a closed or open manner, thus influencing the capacity of actors to intervene in its defence (*see* Wolford 2004 on the Sem Terra movement in Brazil). From this point of view, in both the valley and the Straits images are constructed of "open" and inclusive spaces rather than "closed" courtyard.

In the mentioned document, the appeal to "defend the territory as a precious common good for everyone and not just for the community that resides in it" recalls this open image of territory, and sees protesters defend the value of use ("precious common good") against the value of exchange ("resource to exploit and violate"). This seems to confirm the approach to local conflicts as opposing residents against developers. In our analysis of these two protest campaigns we have underlined, however, how interests and identity in the territory are reconstructed in action. The identification of many residents with the value of use (or in contrast the value of exchange) of the territory does not derive from an interest as given. It occurs instead through a long process of giving symbolic significance to the conflict, in the course of which there emerges a positive conception of communitarian identity that recalls universal values, as well as a definition of the conflict that extends from the local to the global level, with the claim to be defending the "common good" against the particularistic advantages promised by the promoters of large-scale infrastructural projects. The No Tav and No Bridge movements reject the accusations of Nimbyism advanced by the promoters of these large-scale public works (i.e. to be conservative actors in favour of egotistical interests rather than the common good) and instead identify the community and territory as common resources that should not be the object of exclusive ownership. This definition of the common good emerges in the course of both protests, intertwining the proposals and concerns of the actors involved and linking them in a protest network: defence of the environment and "ungrowth" proposed by environmental associations; "good jobs" suggested by militant trade unionists; construction of free spaces advanced by the social centres; sovereignty of the local periphery against the national centre supported by the local mayors; social justice and democracy from below as on the agenda of the "movement of movements" (della Porta et al. 2006). The various sources used for our research (documents, interviews with activists, websites, etc.) indicated that the definition of what is at stake in these conflicts supersedes the classic struggle between environmental defence and economic development, proposing instead an alternative model of progress. The struggles against the bridge and the Tav are viewed by participants not only as the defence of a territory's natural heritage and the well-being of its citizens, but also as being oriented towards a future model of development radically different from that proposed by the promoters of large-scale public works, criticised here for being exclusively concerned with the interests of investors, the logic of profit and the exploitation of common goods for private use. In this sense, during the campaigns we observe a geographical scale shift, as well as the development of cross-issue bridges.

If what is at stake becomes symbolically defined during the course of action, the two protest campaigns cannot be described as purely reactive in opposing decisions "taken elsewhere", but become constructive through the many proposals they advance. These alternative proposals are often very specific (e.g. modernising the rail infrastructure already existent in Val di Susa, improving the transport system in Sicily and Calabria) and oriented towards what activists define as an "alternative notion of development, based on the real needs of a territory and its population, on the concern for the common good and the growth of social solidarity" (DME 27), as well as the development of locally rooted economies. This model of "ungrowth" is based on defence of the environment, employment and quality of life in the territory, with an increasingly "radical criticism of the current model of development". Even from a strictly economic viewpoint, those who contest large-scale public works criticise the waste of public money (their promoters usually claim these are "zero cost" and financed entirely from private sources) and suggest alternative ways in which these public resources can be used. At the centre of this symbolic conflict is the conception of a general interest that the opponents of these projects claim to interpret, while accusing the promoters of defending the particularistic interests of corrupt speculators in Val di Susa (on corruption in high-speed railway projects, *see* Imposimato et al. 1999) or of Mafia organisations and construction cartels in the area of the Straits (Mangano and Mazzeo 2006).

Through this symbolic construction of conflict the activists develop motivational frames by stressing the real possibility of affecting decisions "taken elsewhere", not only by mobilising citizens against specific modalities of these projects but also by encouraging them to contest whether or not they should be undertaken at all. What is at stake in these conflicts is also a meta-discourse on democracy. This is conceived not only as the right to protest but also as the right of the local population (together with the local politicians that represent them) to decide on large-scale public works that affect their territory, contesting decision-making procedures that are imposed "from above". This demand for greater democracy extends further to advance a different form of democracy, based more on direct participation than on delegated representation. As activists declare: "In all these struggles the re-emergence of communitarian and municipal values brought about the possibility to invent new forms of democracy and self-government, local but in a continual search for open relations and solutions" (DME 27). The conception of politics proposed is based on the direct participation of citizens and the use of local knowledge, rather than the bureaucratic-professional knowledge of delegated institutions and 'expert' groups. It resonates therefore with contemporary conceptions of deliberative democracy (della Porta 2005b).

This research broadly confirms our initial hypothesis: through participation in protest local discourses become global ones, or, as the report puts it: "local and global together" (DME 27). Proposals are advanced here for alternative models of development and a different conception of the general interest, with the protest becoming an example of politics "from below" that experiments with new forms of participatory democracy. This occurs through the adherence to protest networks of diverse political and social actors, who link their interpretative schemes in a common and more general discourse, which intertwines with the mobilisation of the movement for a globalisation from below. In a similar vein, other studies in Europe have found that many local environmental protests "have little to do with Nimby egocentrism" (Larringa and Barcena 2006: 1), "acquiring in many cases a social movement dimension" (Di Masso Tarditti 2006: 1) and becoming part of the movement against a neoliberal globalisation (Graeme 2006). This emphasises the importance of analysing individual protest campaigns in their interaction with broader cycles of protest, highlighting moments in which non-conventional collective actions intensify and diffuse to diverse actors through processes of imitation and learning (Tarrow 1994). What facilitates an upward scale shift is the plurality of actors present in the campaigns, as well as the presence of global frames.

Our two protest campaigns are promoted by socially and politically heterogeneous actors, linked by multiple belonging and "networked" in the course of action, thus producing further waves of mobilisation. Protest campaigns have been described as "a series of thematic, social and temporal interactions that become interconnected, the actors involved believing them to be oriented to a specific objective" (della Porta and Rucht 2002: 3). In the course of our two campaigns, this participation extended to diverse social groups, ideological viewpoints and different generations, involving and redefining the local community while remaining open to external actors. The types of collective actors that form into networks, bringing their respective resources and skills, are very similar in Val di Susa and the area of the Straits, although their relative weight and modes of interaction are rather different.

In line with the interpretation of local conflicts as environmental actions, the spontaneous citizens' committees and the national environmental associations play a fundamental role in both protest campaigns, confirming the findings of recent studies on these collective actors. In particular, our research has indicated that, while the environmental movement institutionalised and moderated its forms of protest in the 1990s, in the following decade environmental associations began to link defence of the environment to the theme of global justice, thus moving away from being single-issue organisations. The environmental associations are important actors here, particularly in the initial and incubating phases of protest, bringing technical-scientific knowledge and public legitimacy, as well as developing informational and procedural strategies. However, tensions have emerged with more radical actors in the movement, not only because environmental associations are often seen as single-issue by the latter, but also because the former tend to favour transversal alliances with institutional actors from right to left of the political spectrum.

The citizens' committees (typical actors in local conflicts) are one of the resources of the Val di Susa protest, while in the Straits they are also significant but less numerous and influential. Their influence can be partly attributed to their capacity to activate pre-existing networks of citizens (mobilised in response to earlier protest campaigns), as well as their ability to mobilise otherwise non-protesting residents. Although weakly organised, sometimes unstable and occasionally discontinued, these "spontaneous" actors demonstrate at times great capacities of mobilisation, are strongly rooted in their territory, and are able to interconnect between different actors on specific themes, precisely because of their participative and flexible structure. As in other cases (for instance, the anti-nuclear protest in Germany, see Rucht 1980), citizens' committees tend to evolve from local and fragmented actors into organisationally coordinated groups, which are direct action-oriented and advance a general discourse on environment and democracy.

Yet the real novelty of our local protests with a global reach is the active presence of other groups that are often absent or play only a marginal role in such protests, from social centres and militant unions to local mayors. If earlier studies (e.g. against the high speed railways in France; Lolive 1999) have already noted the participation of groups that were not formed by (or exclusively focused on) the protest itself, in our two cases the protest network is particularly vast and heterogeneous.

The activists of the squatted social centres and the "antagonistic" area have brought our two protest campaigns generational resources (young, mainly students), political-organisational resources (through the diffusion of No Tav and No Bridge themes outside the local dimension) and repertoires of action (countercultural activities, creative demonstrations, direct actions) developed during the earlier occupation of autonomous spaces. Although often seen as violent by the mass media and the authorities (hence "uncomfortable" allies for other protesters), the social centres soon become key actors in mobilising both protests. In fact, their activists immediately promote initiatives in the No Bridge campaign that help to develop networks and coordination (despite their usual distrust of political parties and associations), while in the No Tav campaign they integrate into existing networks by participating in protests and developing bonds of mutual trust with other actors. The presence of social centres brings elements of internal tension to the movement (although rare and mainly in the area of the Straits), particularly with respect to the political parties and environmental associations involved. Yet differences emerge more over broader strategies to adopt and differing conceptions of democratic participation than over specific repertoires of action.

While the main Italian unions (CGIL, CISL, UIL) are generally in favour of large-scale public works (with the exception of the more radical wing of CGIL), militant unions have been key actors in both campaigns, involving sectors of workers in these mobilisations and linking defence of the environment to public health and employment, while opposing privatisation in public services and transport. The active presence of social centres and militant unions in both campaigns highlights the ways in which the mobilisation against large-scale public works has become intertwined with the broader movement for a globalisation from below, of which both militant unions and social centres form an integral part, especially in the Italian case (Andretta et al. 2002). It is due in large part to these actors and their frames that the struggle against large-scale public works becomes part of a wider opposition to the model of development proposed by neoliberal globalisation.

Local politicians (both in the Communes and the Mountainous Communities) represent a key and innovative node of the protest network. Although past experiences of local mobilisation on environmental issues have seen local governments form temporary alliances with protest committees (especially in rural or peripheral areas), this strategy has met with the accusation of Nimey ('not in my electoral yard'), because of the perceived electoral benefits for politicians involved (Lascoumes 1994: 233). However, these cases differ from other territorial conflicts because the border between protesters and institutional actors is rather fluid, given that mayors and presidents of Mountainous Communities form an integral part of the No Tav protest, while local mayors are less relevant in the No Bridge campaign. These actors bring to the movement important resources of public legitimacy, integrate into existing networks, and build bonds of mutual trust with other actors through actions of contestation.

Our perspective on these protest campaigns has underlined the dynamics of interaction through which a "narrative of the conflict is built, whose individual stages can only be understood by reference to earlier protests, and the interests or identity of the diverse actors involved" (della Porta and Rucht 2002). If the interests and identities of diverse actors often undergo reciprocal tensions (Griggs and Howarth 2002), we have seen that the success of the protest campaigns in both Val di Susa and the Straits is tied to the capacity of reciprocal crossfertilisation between actors. The success of mobilisation facilitates the development of cooperative links between different protest actors, who tend to compete in the subsiding phase of protest (della Porta and Tarrow 2005). If resources have traditionally been seen as pre-existing the action itself, our analysis has underlined the formation of resources in action.

Our analysis of these campaigns also confirms the importance of political opportunities. Existing literature on social movements has chronicled the intensification of protest when channels of access to authority open, institutional alliances emerge and divisions occur within the elite. Our research has shown the importance of the participation of local political actors, often in conflict with governing parties at national and regional level, as well as the different strategies adopted during the opening and closing of policy windows. In particular, protest intensified when the decision-making process accelerates (Objective Law, tender for a General Contractor) as well as in the phase of implementation (start of building works in Val di Susa). These "windows of opportunity" have been successfully exploited by protest actors (both institutional and otherwise) who are able to intervene in processes of policy-making at various levels and give visibility to the protest. Yet the local dimension is not isolated from other territorial levels, as all the actors involved play a multi-level game. Particularly in Val di Susa, the development of a transnational project facilitates the interactions with French organisations from the start of the protest. In both campaigns the transnational dimension is most relevant at European level, largely because the EU is involved in the financing and implementation of these projects. The European institutions therefore became a key target for the protest, as well as an arena in which to find allies, the latter occurring in particular at the European Parliament (della Porta and Caiani 2006).

With respect to political opportunities, our research has confirmed the weakening capacity of political parties to mediate in conflicts between centre and periphery, which in turn have become increasingly disruptive (*see* also della Porta 2004b). If the small parties of the radical left (the Communist PRC and PdCI, as well as the Greens) were involved in these protests, the large parties of both centre-left and centre-right are generally in support of large-scale public projects and here become targets of protest. These parties are seen as increasingly distant and unable to represent the needs of the local population at higher institutional levels (regional, national, European), where decisions taken are viewed as being "imposed from above". The public decision-making process for the Tav and the Bridge is perceived within the community as a violation of the competences of the local level in a politically decentralised system, given that most of the locally elected politicians are against these projects. Furthermore, it is seen as an expression of inefficiency and inadequacy in the mechanisms of representative democracy, against which protesters propose an alternative model of local democracy based on the direct participation of citizens. In this sense the conflicts over the Tav and the bridge can be located within the framework of research on new forms of democracy, confronting the challenges of a decision-making process that is moving above national states to the international level, as well as a popular response to free market politics (della Porta and Tarrow 2005).

Yet No Tav and No Bridge protesters do not limit themselves to demanding a different kind of democracy, but seek to develop and practise this in the course of their protest actions, through the construction of networked organisational structures and the adoption of inclusive decision-making mechanisms.

As in other types of collective mobilisations, in our two campaigns the "social capital" inherent in different types of networked associations grew in the course of action, through the meeting and crossfertilisation of diverse actors on different themes. Mayors and environmentalists, committees and social centres, militant unions and student collectives are all part of a network that coordinates the protests, albeit with different modalities and characteristics in the two campaigns. In Val di Susa the coordination of local politicians, committees, associations and social centres takes the form of extensive, stable networks with an assembly-like structure, a deliberative organisational model, and a consensual method of decision-making, based on the search for choices and decisions that have the broadest possible support. These structures *see* a very high level of participation. Although the assembly system might delay the decision-making process, it is very positive in terms of constructing a collective identity. In this sense we *see* in both Val di Susa and the Straits a stress on the tolerance of diversity, perceived as an asset rather than a limit to mobilisation, a feature already observed in the social forum (della Porta 2005a).

In the area of the Straits, numerous coordinations and networks succeed each other chronologically and diversify spatially (between the Sicilian and Calabrian coasts), adopting a more informal structure than in Val di Susa. They often meet ad hoc for specific initiatives, with a small nucleus of activists assuring the continuity of mobilisation, although the names of the organisations involved may change. Another difference with the No Tav is that the organisational process is more territorially decentralised and the decision-making process is characterised by negotiation within a small group of individual activists who prepare the larger initiatives. The increasing participation of ordinary citizens in organised demonstrations does not extend to participation in organised networks, the latter being constituted by geographically diverse components (Messina and Calabria) and political viewpoints (moderate and radical), with an organisational dynamic that oscillates between cooperation and conflict, the search for unity in action and the recognition of internal divisions.

The differences that emerge in the course of these two protest campaigns have a number of possible explanations. First, there is a different political and associational context: the high intensity of "social capital" in Val di Susa, due to the presence of a strong leftist subculture with a tradition of association and participation, may explain the greater involvement of ordinary people in the No Tav campaign, while the delegation of protest organisation to core activists in the No Bridge campaign may result from the weaker traditions of protest and lower levels of association in the area of the Straits. In addition, the political opportunities differ in the two campaigns: while in Val di Susa the protests have the strong support of local institutions, contrasting with the bipartisan support for the Tav at regional and national level, in the area of the Straits strong political divisions emerge over the project at both local and national levels.

However, political opportunities and pre-existing networked associations are not sufficient to explain the different organisational paths of the two protests. As we suggested in the introductory chapter, in order to reconstruct the evolution of the protest campaigns within a framework that recognises the transforming value of action, we should note the capacity of specific events to interrupt the routine of protest and challenge existing structures. Certain phases of the protest cycle, in particular those with intense mobilisation in response to specific events, witness a process of crossfertilisation in action through organisational networking and the multiplication of individual belonging. This occurs in Val di Susa during the site occupations of 2005, with the violent evacuation of protesters by the police and the reoccupation of the site by the former, a struggle that is given greater urgency by the proposed start of the implementation phase of public decision-making (opening of construction site and first ground tests). As in other campaigns around large-scale infrastructural projects – such as nuclear plants or airports – interactions around specific places became more and more symbolically loaded.[1]

The perception of an imminent danger and the involvement of the entire movement in this direct action, as well as the sense of injustice caused by the (military-like) aggression of a (peaceful) community, allow these site occupations to become a deliberative arena that favours the construction of a shared identity, stimulates linkages between the specific frames of diverse actors, and creates feelings of mutual trust and solidarity between participants. A comparable event has not occurred in the area of the Straits, perhaps because the decision-making process is ongoing and the implementation phase remains distant. This has led to the prevalence of informational, symbolic and demonstrative forms of protest in the Straits, which have not yet been challenged by repressive actions. We have nevertheless hypothesised that, should building works go ahead, an intensification of protest may lead to disruptive direct actions, which would facilitate the creation of more coherent and stable networks, as occurred in Val di Susa.

The protest campaigns against the Tav and the bridge were ongoing in 2006 and 2007, although they lost some of the public visibility gained in the preceding year. This can be attributed to the partial success of both protests. In Val di Susa the implementation phase has been temporarily blocked and building sites removed, although the new centre-left Prodi government has maintained an ambiguous position, affirming the centrality of the high-speed network while seeking an agreement with the local population. In the area of the Straits the public decision-making process has formally concluded, with a contract signed between SdM and a General Contractor; yet the implementation phase has been halted because the bridge does not figure as a priority of the new national government. However, the centre-right Regional President of Sicily (Toto Cuffaro) has publicly announced that the works will go ahead even without the assent of the Prodi government (Si 22/7/06).

A question remains as to whether we can predict how these two protest campaigns will evolve in the future. A lot depends on the decisions taken by the national government. If the implementation phase in either project goes ahead then protests are likely to intensify again and the conflict will become visible and possibly more radical. If the two projects are abandoned, the campaign is likely to demobilise, leaving behind a wealth of ideas and experiences of collective action, which can be reactivated in new local mobilisations with a global reach. While protest campaigns are often favoured by an environment with high levels of "social capital", they can also prove capable of creating and consolidating a "critical" social capital that provides the resources for new mobilisations (Tarrow 2000; della Porta and Diani 2006).

While future institutional decision-making will affect the nature of either protest, much will also depend on the continued capacity of both No Tav and No Bridge activists to voice strong signals of dissent from the valley and the Straits to institutional decision-makers in Rome and elsewhere.

Note

1. For example, the conflicts around the construction of the airport Tokyo-Narita (Apter and Sawa 1984) or the enlargement of the Frankfurt airport (Rucht 1984).

Bibliography

Allasino, E. 2004. "Tra il cortile di casa e il network: la struttura organizzativa interna", in D. della Porta (ed.), *Comitati di cittadini e democrazia urbana*. Soveria Mannelli: Rubbettino, pp. 43–70.

Andretta, M. 2004. "L'identità dei comitati tra egoismo e bene pubblico", in D. della Porta (ed.), *Comitati di cittadini e democrazia urbana*. Soveria Mannelli: Rubbettino, pp. 71–96.

Andretta, M., D. della Porta, L. Mosca, and H. Reiter. 2002. *Global, noglobal, new global. La protesta contro il G8 a Genova*. Rome-Bari: Laterza.

Apter, D. and N. Sawa. 1984. *Against the State. Politics and Social Protest in Japan*. Cambridge, Mass.: Harvard University Press.

Bettini, V., M. Guerzoni and A. Ziparo. (eds). 2002. *Il ponte insostenibile. L'impatto ambientale del manufatto di attraversamento stabile dello Stretto di Messina*. Florence: Alinea Editrice.

Bobbio, L. 1999. "Un processo equo per una localizzazione equa", in L. Bobbio and A. Zeppetella (eds), *Perché proprio qui? Grandi opere e opposizioni locali*. Milan: Franco Angeli, pp. 185–237.

Bobbio, L. and A. Zeppetella (eds). 1999. *Perché proprio qui? Grandi opere e opposizioni locali*. Milan: Franco Angeli.

Borelli, G. 1999. "Davide contro Golia. L'inceneritore Fenice a Verrone", in L. Bobbio and A. Zeppetella (eds), *Perché proprio qui? Grandi opere e opposizioni locali*. Milan: Franco Angeli, pp. 15–52.

Buso, G. 1996. "Resistenze e proteste contro le decisioni del governo locale: i comitati spontanei di cittadini", in L. Bobbio and F. Ferraresi (eds), *Decidere in Comune, Analisi e riflessioni su cento decisioni comunali*. Turin: Fondazione Rosselli, pp. 126–41.

Clemens, E.S. 2005. "Two Kinds of Stuff: the Current Encounter of Social Movements and Organizations", in G.F. Davis, D. McAdam, W.R. Scott and M.N. Zald (eds), *Social Movements and Organizational Theory*. Cambridge Studies in Contentious Politics. Cambridge, New York: Cambridge University Press, pp. 351–65.

Clemens, E.S. and D.C. Minkoff. 2004. "Beyond the Iron Law: Rethinking the Place of Organizations in Social Movement Research", in D.A. Snow, S.A. Soule and H. Kriesi (eds), *The Blackwell Companion to Social Movements*. Malden, Mass., Oxford: Blackwell Publishing, pp. 155–70.

D'Arcus, B. 2006. *Boundaries of Dissent. Protest and State Power in the Media Age*. New York: Routledge.

della Porta, D. 1995. *Social Movements, Political Violence and the State.* Cambridge, New York: Cambridge University Press.

————. 1999. "Protest, Protesters and Protest Policing", in M. Giugni, D. McAdam and C. Tilly (eds), *How Movements Matter.* Minneapolis: University of Minnesota Press, pp. 66–96.

————. 2003a. "Social Movements and Democracy at the Turn of the Millennium", in P. Ibarra (ed.), *Social Movements and Democracy.* New York: Palgrave Macmillan, pp. 105–36.

————. 2003b. *I new global.* Bologna: il Mulino.

————. 2004a. "Comitati di cittadini e democrazia urbana: una introduzione", in D. della Porta (ed.), *Comitati di cittadini e democrazia urbana.* Soveria Mannelli: Rubbettino, pp. 7–41.

————. 2004b. "Tra democrazia partecipativa e domanda di rappresentanza", in D. della Porta (ed.), *Comitati di cittadini e democrazia urbana,* Soveria Mannelli: Rubbettino, pp. 97–136.

————. 2005a. "Multiple Belongings, Tolerant Identities, and the Construction of Another Politics: Between the European Social Forums and the Local Social Fora", in D. della Porta and S. Tarrow (eds), *Transnational Protest and Global Activism.* Lanham: Rowman and Littlefield, pp. 175–202.

————. 2005b. "Making the Polis: Social Forums and Democracy in the Global Justice Movements", *Mobilization,* 10(1): 73–94.

————. 2006. "From Corporatist Union to Protest Unions? On the (Difficult) Relations Between Organized Labour and New Social Movements", in C. Crouch and W. Streek (eds), *The Diversity of Democracy. Corporatism, Social Order and Political Conflict.* Cheltenham: Edward Elgar, pp. 71–97.

————. 2008. "Case Selection in Case-oriented versus Variable-oriented Research", in D. della Porta and M. Keating (eds), *Approaches and Methods in the Social Sciences.* Cambridge: Cambridge University Press.

della Porta, D. and M. Andretta. 2002. "Changing Forms of Environmentalism in Italy: The Protest Campaign on the High Speed Railway System", *Mobilization,* 7: 59–77.

della Porta, D. and M. Caiani. 2006. *Quale Europa?* Bologna: Il Mulino.

della Porta, D. and M. Diani. 1997. *I movimenti sociali.* Roma: Carocci (in English: *Social Movements: An Introduction.* Oxford, Blackwell, 1999).

della Porta, D. and M. Diani (in collaboration with M. Andretta). 2004. *Movimenti senza protesta? L'ambientalismo in Italia.* Bologna: il Mulino.

della Porta, D. and M. Diani. 2006. *Social Movements: An Introduction,* 2nd edn. Oxford: Blackwell.

della Porta, D. and M. Keating. 2008. 'How Many Paradigms in the Social Sciences? An Epistemological Introduction", in D. della Porta and M. Keating (eds), *Approaches and Methods in the Social Sciences.* Cambridge: Cambridge University Press.

della Porta, D. and L. Mosca. 2006. "Ricercando la rete. Uso di Internet e movimento globale", *Rassegna Italiana di Sociologia*, Special issue on "E-Democracy: Internet e Democrazia", edited by D. della Porta, 47(4): 529–56.

della Porta, D. and L. Mosca. 2007. "In movimento. Contamination in Action and the Italian Global Justice Movement", *Global Networks: a Journal of Transnational Affairs*, 7(1): 1–28.

della Porta, D. and G. Piazza. 2007. "Local Contention, Global Framing: the Protest Campaigns against the TAV in Val di Susa and Bridge on the Messina Straits", *Environmental Politics*, Special issue on "Acting Locally: Local Environmental Mobilisations and Campaigns", edited by C. Rootes, 16(5): 864–882.

della Porta, D. and H. Reiter. 2006. "Conclusion". in D. della Porta, A. Petersen and H. Reiter (eds), *Policing Transnational Protest*. Aldershot: Ashgate, pp. 175–189.

della Porta, D. and D. Rucht. 2002. "The Dynamics of Environmental Campaigns", in D. della Porta and D. Rucht (guest editors), *Comparative Environmental Campaigns*, special issue of *Mobilization*, 7: 1–14.

della Porta, D. and S. Tarrow (eds). 2005. *Transnational Protest and Global Activism*. New York: Rowman and Littlefield.

della Porta, D., M. Andretta, L. Mosca and H. Reiter. 2006. *Globalization from Below. Transnational Activists and Protest Networks*. Minneapolis: University of Minnesota Press.

Diani, M. 1995. *Green Networks. A Structural Analysis of the Italian Environmental Movement*. Edinburgh: Edinburgh University Press.

DiMaggio, P.J. and W.W. Powell. 1991. "Introduction", in W.W. Powell and P.J. DiMaggio (eds), *The New Institutionalism in Organizational Analysis*. Chicago, London: University of Chicago Press, pp. 1–38.

Di Masso Tarditti, A. 2006. "Towards a New Topology of Social-environmental Conflicts: Rethinking NIMBY in the Context of Environmental Mobilisations in Catalonia", paper presented at the *European Consortium for Political Research Joint Sessions of Workshop, 25–30 April 2006*. Nicosia: Intercollege.

Downing, J.D.H. 2001. *Radical Media. Rebellious Communication and Social Movements*. London: Sage.

Eliasoph, N. 1998. *Avoiding Politics: How Americans Produce Apathy in Everyday Life*. New York: Cambridge University Press.

Elkin, S. 1987. *City and Regime*. Chicago: University of Chicago Press.

Fantasia, R. 1988. *Cultures of Solidarity. Consciousness, Action, and Contemporary American Workers*. Berkeley, Calif., London: University of California Press.

Fillieule, O. and M. Jimenez. 2003. "The Methodology of Protest Event Analysis and the Media Politics of Reporting Environmental Protest Event", in C. Rootes (ed), *Environmental Mobilization in Comparative Perspective*. Oxford: Oxford University Press, pp. 258–280.

Gamson, W.A. 1988. "Political Discourse and Collective Action", *International Journal of Social Movements, Conflicts and Change*, 1: 219–44.
————. 1990. *The Strategy of Social Protest*, 2nd edn. Belmont, Calif.: Wadsworth (original edn. 1975).

Gitlin, T. 1980. The Whole World is Watching: Mass Media in the Making and Unmaking of the New Left. Berkeley, Los Angeles, Calif.: University of California Press.

Gordon, C. and J.M. Jasper. 1996. "Overcoming the 'Nimby' Label: Rhetorical and Organizational Links for Local Protestors", *Research in Social Movements, Conflict and Change*, 19: 159–81.

Gould, K.A., A. Schnaiberg and A.S. Weinberg. 1996. *Local Environmental Struggles. Citizen Activism in the Treadmill of Production*. Cambridge: Cambridge University Press.

Graeme, H. 2006. "From Symbolism to Resistance: Anti-GM Actions in France", paper presented at the *European Consortium for Political Research Joint Sessions of Workshop, 25–30 April 2006*. Nicosia: Intercollege.

Griggs, S. and D. Howarth. 2002. "An Alliance of Interest and Identity? Explaining the Campaign against Manchester Airport's Second Runway", in D. della Porta and D. Rucht (guest editors), *Comparative Environmental Campaigns*, special issue of *Mobilization*, 7(1): 43–58.

Halpern, C. 2006. "La décision publique entre intérêt général et intérêt territorialisés. Les conflits sur l'extension des aéroports Paris – Charles de Gaulle et Berlin – Schoenefeld", Ph.D. dissertation. Paris: Fondation Nationale des Sciences Politiques.

Hunt, S., R.D. Benford and D.A. Snow. 1994. "Identity Fields: Framing Processes and the Social Construction of Movement Identities", in E. Laraña, H. Johnston and J. Gusfield (eds), *New Social Movements*. Philadelphia: Temple University Press.

Imposimato, F., G. Pisauro and E. Provvisionato. 1999. *Corruzione ad alta velocità*. Rome: Koiné.

Jasper, J.M. 1997. *The Art of Moral Protest: Culture, Creativity and Biography in Social Movements*. Chicago: Chicago University Press.

Jobert, A. 1998. "L'aménagement en politique- ou ce que la syndrome NIMBY nous dit de l'intérêt général", *Politix*, 42: 67–92.

Johnston, H. 2005. "Comparative Frame Analysis", in H. Johnston and J. Noakes (eds), *Frames of Protest. Social Movements and the Framing Perspective*. Lanham: Boulder, pp. 217–36.

Kitschelt, H. 2003. "Landscape of Political Interest Intermediation: Social Movements, Interest Groups, and Parties in the Early Twenty-first Century", in P. Ibarra (ed.), *Social Movements and Democracy*. New York: Palgrave Macmillan, pp. 81–104.

Kriesi, H. 1996. "The Organizational Structure of New Social Movements in a Political Context", in D. McAdam, J.D. McCarthy and M.N. Zald (eds),

Comparative Perpectives on Social Movements: Political Opportunities, Mobilizing Structures and Cultural Framings. New York: Cambridge University Press, pp. 152–84.

Larringa, J. and I. Barcena. 2006. "Beyond the NIMBY Syndrome. Global Dimensions of Local Environmental Activism in the Basque Country", paper presented at the *European Consortium for Political Research Joint Sessions of Workshop, 25–30 April 2006.* Nicosia: Intercollege.

Lascoumes, P. 1994. *L'Éco-pouvoir. Environnements et politiques.* Paris: Edition La Découverte.

Le Galès, P. 2003. *Le Retour des villes européennes.* Paris: Presses de Sciences Po.

Levine, M. 1989. "The Politics of Partnership. Urban Redevelopment since 1945", in G. Squires (ed.), *Unequal Partnership.* New Brunswick, NJ: Rutgers University Press, pp. 12–34.

Lewanski, R. 2004. "Il discorso della protesta", in D. della Porta (ed.), *Comitati di cittadini e democrazia urbana.* Soveria Mannelli: Rubbettino, pp. 199–230.

Lindblom, C. 1980. *The Policy-making Process.* Englewood Cliffs: Prentice Hall.

Lipsky, M. 1965. *Protest in City Politics.* Chicago: Rand McNally.

Logan, J.R. and H.L. Molotch. 1987. *Urban Fortunes. The Political Economy of Place.* Berkeley: University of California.

Lolive, J. 1999. *Les Contestations du TGV Méditerranée: projet, controversies et espace publique.* Paris: L'Harmattan.

Mangano, A. and A. Mazzeo. 2006. *Il mostro sullo Stretto. Sette ottimi motivi per non costruire il Ponte.* Ragusa: Sicilia Punto L, terrelibere.org.

Margaira, O. 2005. *Adesso o mai più.* Borgone Susa: Edizioni del Graffio.

McAdam, D., S. Tarrow and C. Tilly. 2003. *The Politics of Contention.* New York: Cambridge University Press.

McCarthy, J.D. and M.N. Zald. 1987. "Resource Mobilization and Social Movements: a Partial Theory", in M.N. Zald and J.D. McCarthy (eds), *Social Movements in an Organizational Society.* New Brunswick, NJ, Oxford: Transaction Books, pp. 15–42.

McCarthy, J.D., J. Smith and M.N. Zald. 1996. "Accessing Public, Media, Electoral, and Governmental Agendas', in D. McAdam, J.D. McCarthy and M.N. Zald (eds), *Comparative Perpectives on Social Movements: Political Opportunities, Mobilizing Structures and Cultural Framings.* New York: Cambridge University Press, pp. 291–311.

Oliver, P. and H. Johnston. 2005. "What a Good Idea. Idea and Frames in Social Movement Research", in H. Johnston and J. Noakes (eds), *Frames of Protest. Social Movements and the Framing Perspective.* Lanham: Boulder, pp. 185–204.

Ortoleva, P. 1988. *Saggio sui Movimenti del 68 in Europa e in America.* Rome: Editori Riuniti.

Piazza, G. 2004. "Le risorse dei comitati nei processi decisionali", in D. della Porta (ed.), *Comitati di cittadini e democrazia urbana.* Soveria Mannelli: Rubbettino, pp. 137–70.

————. 2007. "Which Democracy Inside the Radical Sector of the Global Justice Movement? The Italian Social Centres: Squatting in Catania", paper presented at the *European Consortium for Political Research Joint Sessions of Workshop, 11 May 2007*. Helsinki: University of Helsinki.

Pieroni, O. 2002. "Effetti sociali e culturali del Ponte sullo Stretto", in V. Bettini, M. Guerzoni and A. Ziparo (eds), *Il ponte insostenibile. L'impatto ambientale del manufatto di attraversamento stabile dello Stretto di Messina*. Florence: Alinea Editrice, pp. 233–242.

Piven, F.F. and R. Cloward. 1977. *Poor People's Movements*. New York: Pantheon.

Pizzorno, A. 1993. *Le radici della politica assoluta*. Milan: Feltrinelli.

————. 1996. "Mutamenti nelle istituzioni rappresentative e sviluppo dei partiti politici", in AA. VV., *Storia d'Europa. L'età contemporanea*. Turin: Einaudi, pp. 961–1031.

————. 1997. "Le trasformazioni del sistema politico italiano 1976–1992", in F. Barbagallo (ed.), *Storia dell'Italia repubblicana*. Turin: Einaudi, pp. 303–44.

————. 2007. *Il velo della diversità*. Milan: Feltrinelli.

Polletta, F. 2006. *It Was like a Fever*. Chicago: University of Chicago Press.

Rochon, T.R. 1988. *Between Society and State. Mobilizing for Peace in Wesstern Europe*. Princeton: Princeton University Press.

Rochon, T.R. 1998. *Culture Moves. Ideas, Activism, and Changing Values*. Princeton: Princeton University Press.

Rootes, C. 2005. "A Limited Transnationalization? The British Environmental Movement", in D. della Porta and S. Tarrow (eds), *Transnational Protest and Global Activism*. Lanham, Md.: Rowman and Littlefield, pp. 21–43.

Rucht, D. 1980. *Von Wyl nach Gorleben. Buerger gegen Atomprogramm und nukleare Entsorgung*. Munich: Beck.

————. (ed.). 1984. *Flughaven Projekte als Politikum. Die Konflikte in Stuttgart, Muenchen und Frankfurt*. Frankfurt am Main: Campus.

Sasso, C. 2002. *Canto per la nostra valle. Diario fra qualità della vita e prepotenza della velocità*. Turin: Edizioni Morra.

————. 2005. *No Tav. Cronache dalla Val di Susa*. Naples: Intramoenia.

Schlosberg, D. 2002. *Environmental Justice and the New Pluralism*. Oxford: Oxford University Press.

Scott, W.R. 1983. "The Organization of Environments: Networks, Cultural, and Historical Elements", in J.W. Meyer and W.R. Scott (eds), *Organizational Environments. Ritual and Rationality*. Beverly Hills, Calif.: Sage, pp. 155–75.

Sebastiani, C. 2001. "Comitati di cittadini e spazi pubblici urbani", *Rassegna Italiana di Sociologia*, 42: 77–114.

Sewell, W.H. 1996. "Three Temporalities: Toward an Eventful Sociology", in T.J. McDonald (ed.), *The Historic Turn in the Human Science*. Ann Arbor: University of Michigan Press, pp. 245–80.

Smith, J., J. McCarthy, C. McPhail and A. Boguslaw. 2001. "From Protest to Agenda Building: Description Bias in Media Coverage of Protest Events in Washington D.C.", *Social Forces*, 79: 1397–423.

Snow, D.A. and R.D. Benford. 1988. "Ideology, Frame Resonance, and Participant Mobilization", *International Social Movement Research*, 1: 197–217.

Snow, D.A., B.E. Rochford, S. Worden and R. Benford. 1986. "Frame Alignment Processes, Micromobilization, and Movement Participation", *American Sociological Review*, 51: 464–81.

Stone, C. 1993. "Urban Regimes and the Capacity to Govern", *Journal of Urban Affairs*, 15: 1–28.

Tarrow, S. 1994. *Power in Movement. Social Movements, Collective Action and Politics*. New York, Cambridge: Cambridge University Press.

————. 2000. "Mad Cows and Social Activists: Contentious Politics in the Trilateral Democracies", in R. Putnam, S. Pharr and R.D. Putnam (eds), *Disaffected Democracies. What's Troubling the Trilateral Countries*. Princeton: Princeton University Press, pp. 270–310.

Tarrow, S. and D. McAdam. 2005. "Scale Shift in Transnational Contention", in D. della Porta and S. Tarrow (eds), *Transnational Protest and Global Activism*. Lanham, Md.: Rowman and Littlefield, pp. 121–44.

Taylor, V. and N. van Dyke. 2004. 'Get Up, Stand up'. Tactical Repertoires of Social Movements", in D. Snow, S.A. Soule and H. Kriesi (eds), *The Blackwell Companion to Social Movements*. Oxford: Blackwell, pp. 262–293.

Thomas, J.C. and H. Savitch. 1991. "Introduction: Big City Politics, Then and Now", in H. Savitch and J.C. Thomas, *Big City Politics in Transition*. Newbury Park, Calif.: Sage, pp. 1–13.

Tilly, C. 1978. *From Mobilization to Revolution*. Reading, Mass.: Addison-Wesley.

————. 1986. *The Contentious French*. Cambridge, Mass.: Harvard University Press.

Touraine, A., F. Dubet, Z. Hegedus and M. Wieviorka. 1981. *Le Pays contre L'état. Luttes occitanes*. Paris: Seuil.

Touraine, A., Z. Hegedus, F. Dubet and M. Wieviorka. 1983. *Anti-nuclear Protest. The Opposition to Nuclear Power in France*. Cambridge: Cambridge University Press.

Trom, D. 1999. "De la réfutation de l'effet NIMBY considérée comme une pratique militante. Notes pour une approche pragmatique de l'activité revendicative", *Revue française de sciences politique*, 49: 31–50.

Vallocchi, S. 2005. "Collective Action Frames in the Gay Liberation Movement", in H. Johnston and J. Noakes (eds), *Frames of Protest. Social Movements and the Framing Perspective*. Lanham: Boulder, pp. 53–68.

Velleità Alternative. 2006. "No Tav. La valle che resiste", special issue of *Autonomia*, 15.

Williams, B.A. and A.R. Matheny. 1995. *Democracy, Dialogue and Environmental Disputes. The Contested Languages of Social Regulation*. New Haven: Yale University Press.

Wilson, J. 1973. *Introduction to Social Movements*. New York: Basic Books.

Wolford, W. 2004. "This Land Is Ours Now: Spatial Imaginaries and the Struggle for Land in Brazil", *Annals of the Association of American Geographers*, 94: 409–24.

Zald, M.N. and J.D. McCarthy. 1987. "Introduction", in M.N. Zald and J.D. McCarthy (eds), *Social Movements in an Organizational Society*. New Brunswick, NJ, Oxford: Transaction Books, pp. 45–47.

Interviews

Interviews on the Straits (carried out by Gianni Piazza)

IME 1. Interview with A. Giordano, responsible for the protected areas of the WWF, Messina, 9/5/05.

IME 2. Interview with C. Pigneri, Coordinamento "CariddiScilla" – Ds, Messina, 9/5/05.

IME 3. Interview with S. Visicaro, comitato "La Nostra Città" – "Messinasenzaponte", Messina, 14/5/05.

IME 4. Interview with M. Camarata, "Laboratorio contro il ponte" – Coordinamento "Rete No Ponte", Messina, 12/12/05.

IME 5. Interview with A. Mazzeo, *Terre Libere*, Messina, 20/4/06.

IME 6. Interview with S. Bonfiglio, provincial secretary Partito della Rifondazione Comunista, Messina, 8/5/06.

IME 7. Interview with M. Marzolla, Coordinamento Calabrese/Meridionale contro il Ponte – ex Centro Sociale "A. Cartella", Reggio Calabria, 18/5/06.

Interviews in Val di Susa (carried out by Massimiliano Andretta and Eugenio Pizzimenti)

IVS 1. Interview with Chiara, Centro Sociale Askatasuna, Val di Susa, 16/2/06.

IVS 2. Interview with Cosimo Scarinzi, secretary of Comitati Unitari di Base, Val di Susa, 18/2/06.

IVS 3. Interview with Gianni De Masi, councillor of Verdi, Val di Susa, 18/2/06.

IVS 4. Interview with Maurizio Piccione, Comitato Spinta dal Bass di Avigliana, Val di Susa, 18/2/06.

IVS 5. Interview with Pierpaolo Coterchio, Legambiente Piemonte, and with Gigi Richetto, university professor, Val di Susa, 17/2/06.

IVS 6. Interview with Orsola Casagrande, journalist *Il Manifesto*, Val di Susa, 16/2/06.

IVS 7. Interview with Mauro Russo, Mayor of Chianocco, Val di Susa, 17/2/06

IVS 8. Interview with Antonio Ferrentino, president of the Comunità Montana Bassa Val Susa, Val di Susa, 17/2/06.

IVS 9. Interview with Marina Clerico, university professor of Environmental Security at Politecnico di Torino, Val di Susa, 17/2/06.

IVS 10. Interview with Nicoletta Dosio, Secretary of the local Circle of Partito della Rifondazione Comunista of Bussoleno-Val di Susa, Val di Susa, 17/2/06.

IVS 11. Interview with Giovanni Vighetti, Comitato di Lotta Popolare contro l'alta velocità di Bussoleno, Val di Susa, 16/2/06.

Documents

DME 1. *"Perché prevalga la saggezza".* Appello del Comitato Tra Scilla e Cariddi – 16/6/1988, in A. D'Agostino (ed.), *Lo Stretto di Messina. Il ponte insostenibile e le sue alternative,* in *Quaderni del sud – quaderni calabresi,* special issue, n° 98–99, December 2005–March 2006.

DME 2. *Petizione Popolare contro la costruzione del Ponte sullo Stretto di Messina per un reale sviluppo della Sicilia.* Comitato La Nostra Città – Messina 3/5/02. www.messinasenzaponte.it

DME 3. *Accoglimento Proposta Del Social Forum Europeo Di Firenze per la realizzazione del Campeggio Internazionale contro il Ponte sullo Stretto da realizzarsi a Messina-Villa S. Giovanni 28 Luglio – 2 Agosto 2003.* Messina Social Forum – Rete del Sud Ribelle – Coordinamento Calabrese contro il Ponte, 1/3/203. www.noponte.org

DME 5. *Appello per la Manifestazione nazionale contro le Grandi Opere, Verona 24/10/2003.* Coordinamento Nazionale Contro le Grandi Opere. www.noponte.org

DME 6. Comunicato stampa – *Convocazione del 2° Campeggio Internazionale contro il Ponte sullo Stretto, 2–8 Agosto 2004.* CSOA "Angelina Cartella", Coordinamento Calabrese contro il Ponte, Network Antagonista Palermitano, Catania Social forum, Laboratorio Autorganizzazione di Messina, Confederazione dei Cobas, Rete del Sud Ribelle. Tutte le realtà presenti al 1° Campeggio Internazionale contro il Ponte. Area dello stretto 18/1/04. www.noponte.org

DME 12. *Il decalogo nero del Ponte sullo Stretto,* 13/10/05, WWF Italia. www.wwf.it.

DME 13. *Documento conclusivo del 4° Corteo nazionale contro il Ponte.* Rete No Ponte 2005, Messina 6/8/05. www.terrelibere.org

DME 16. *Mozione finale dell'Assemblea della Rete Meridionale Nuovo Municipio/No Ponte.* Reggio Calabria, 10 December 2005. www.terrelibere.org

DME 17. *Per il gemellaggio NO TAV – NO PONTE.* Coordinamento No

Ponte – Rete Meridionale del Nuovo Municipio. Reggio Calabria, 29 December 2005. www.retenoponte.org

DME 18. Appello *"TUTTI A MESSINA – 22 gennaio 2006 – PER DIFENDERE LO STRETTO"*. RETE NO PONTE. Messina, 5/1/06. www.messinasenzaponte.it

DME 19. *"10 buone ragioni per dire NO"*. Sintesi delle osservazioni critiche presentate dai Verdi al SIA, in A. D'Agostino (ed.), *Lo Stretto di Messina. Il ponte insostenibile e le sue alternative*, in *Quaderni del sud – quaderni calabresi*, special issue, n°. 98–99, December 2005–March 2006.

DME 20. *"A venti anni dalla battaglia contro la Megacentrale a carbone"*, in A. D'Agostino (ed.), *Lo Stretto di Messina. Il ponte insostenibile e le sue alternative*, in *Quaderni del sud – quaderni calabresi*, special issue, n° 98–99, December 2005–March 2006.

DME 21. *"L'opposizione del popolo dello Stretto. Il referendum anticentrale"*, in A. D'Agostino (ed.), *Lo Stretto di Messina. Il ponte insostenibile e le sue alternative*, in *Quaderni del sud – quaderni calabresi*, special issue, n° 98–99, December 2005–March 2006.

DME 22. Appello *"Campagna Nazionale Boicotta il Ponte"*. Comitato organizzatore Campagna "Boicotta il Ponte", Messina, 14/3/206, www.terrelibere.org.

DME 23. *Fermiamo lo sviluppo del capitale. Documento finale dell'Assemblea plenaria del 1° Campeggio internazionale contro il Ponte sullo Stretto* (Cannitello-Punta Faro, 28 July–2 August 2003), in A. D'Agostino (ed.), *Lo Stretto di Messina. Il ponte insostenibile e le sue alternative*, in *Quaderni del sud – quaderni calabresi*, special issue, n° 98–99, December 2005–March 2006.

DME 25. *La resistenza delle istituzioni del luogo. Dieci domande al sindaco di Villa S. Giovanni*, in A. D'Agostino (ed.), *Lo Stretto di Messina. Il ponte insostenibile e le sue alternative*, in *Quaderni del sud – quaderni calabresi*, special issue, n° 98–99, December 2005–March 2006.

DME 26. *Documento di adesione della CUB di Messina alle mobilitazioni contro il Ponte sullo Stretto*, in A. D'Agostino (ed.), *Lo Stretto di Messina. Il ponte insostenibile e le sue alternative*, in *Quaderni del sud – quaderni calabresi*, special issue, n° 98–99, December 2005–March 2006.

DME 27. *"Grandi Opere? Grandi bidoni!"* Comunicato-mozione approvato dall'Assemblea contro le Grandi Opere, Venice, 11/2/06.

DVS 1. Coordinamento dei comitati no tav valle di susa, Torino e Gronda Ovest, *Il 6 e 7 ottobre a Venaus non devono entrare*, leaflet, 29/9/05.

DVS 2. Appello medici di base valsusini, *TAV: amianto e uranio*, petizione, 30/5/04.

DVS 3. Comunità montana alta Val di Susa, comunità montana bassa Val di Susa, Conferenza dei sindaci della Val di Susa e della "Grotta Ovest" di Torino, Comitati No Tav, Ass. Col diretti, Ass. Montagna Nostra,

Legambiente, WWF, Pronatura, Arci Val di Susa, Associazioni ambientaliste, Sabato *4 giugno 2005: Tutti a Susa*, leaflet.

DVS 5. Petizione dei lavoratori della Val di Susa, *Decidiamo il nostro futuro*, petition.

DVS 6. Coordinamento torinese No Tav ..., *Sabato 17 dicembre: Manifestazione No-Tav a Torino*, leaflet.

DVS 7. Cobas Scuola Torino, *Contro i treni ad alta velocità, sciopero di popolo in Val di Susa*, leaflet, 16/11/05.

DVS 8. Federazione Anarchici Italiani Torino, *Fermiamo il treno della morte*, 11/4/05, leaflet.

DVS 10. No Tav. *Appello degli artisti*, press release, 4/11/05.

DVS 16. Arci et al., Stop subito alla violenza in Val di Susa, no date.

Newspapers

A – *l'Avanti*
CdS – *Corriere della Sera*
GaS – *la Gazzetta del Sud*
GdS– *il Giornale di Sicilia*
Io – *Italia Oggi*
L – *Liberazione*
M – *Il Manifesto*
Me – *Il Messaggero*
R – *La Repubblica*
S – *La Stampa*
Si – *La Sicilia*
U – *L'Unità*

Press Agency

Ansa

Websites

www.cariddiscilla.it
www.messinasenzaponte.it
www.montagnanostra.altervista.org
www.nopontestrettomessina.it
www.pontopoli.it
www.terrelibere.org

www.finanzaonline.com
www.messinasocialforum.it
www.noponte.org
www.notav.it
www.retenoponte.org

Index